Fifth Edition

An Anthology of Indigenous Literatures in English

Voices from Canada

Edited by
**Armand Garnet Ruffo • Katherena Vermette
Daniel David Moses • Terry Goldie**

OXFORD
UNIVERSITY PRESS

Oxford University Press is a department of the University of Oxford.
It furthers the University's objective of excellence in research, scholarship,
and education by publishing worldwide. Oxford is a registered trade mark of
Oxford University Press in the UK and in certain other countries.

Published in Canada by
Oxford University Press
8 Sampson Mews, Suite 204,
Don Mills, Ontario M3C 0H5 Canada

www.oupcanada.com

Copyright © Oxford University Press Canada 2020

The moral rights of the authors have been asserted

Database right Oxford University Press (maker)

First Edition published in 1992
Second Edition published in 1998
Third Edition published in 2005
Fourth Edition published in 2013

All rights reserved. No part of this publication may be reproduced, stored in
a retrieval system, or transmitted, in any form or by any means, without the
prior permission in writing of Oxford University Press, or as expressly permitted
by law, by licence, or under terms agreed with the appropriate reprographics
rights organization. Enquiries concerning reproduction outside the scope of the
above should be sent to the Permissions Department at the address above
or through the following url: www.oupcanada.com/permission/permission_request.php

Every effort has been made to determine and contact copyright holders.
In the case of any omissions, the publisher will be pleased to make
suitable acknowledgement in future editions.

Library and Archives Canada Cataloguing in Publication

Title: An anthology of Canadian Native literature in English : voices from Canada / edited by
Armand Ruffo and Katherena Vermette.
Other titles: Voices from Canada
Names: Ruffo, Armand Garnet, 1955- editor. | Vermette, Katherena, 1977- editor.
Description: Fifth edition. | Includes index.
Identifiers: Canadiana 20190157593 | ISBN 9780199031719 (softcover)
Subjects: LCSH: Indians of North America—Canada—Literary collections. | CSH: Canadian literature
(English)—Indian authors. | CSH: Canadian literature (English)—Inuit authors. | CSH: Canadian
literature (English)—Métis authors.
Classification: LCC PS8235.I6 A56 2020 | DDC C810.8/0897—dc23

Cover and interior design: Sherill Chapman

Oxford University Press is committed to our environment.
Wherever possible, our books are printed on paper which comes from
responsible sources.

Printed and bound in Canada

Contents

A Timeline of Indigenous Literatures xiii
Preface to the Fifth Edition xxi
Introduction xxiii

TRADITIONAL ORATURE 1
Southern First Nations
Song for Medicine Hunting 2
Traditional History of the
 Confederacy 2
Song for the Burning of the
 White Dog 4
Themes: orality, translation, traditional knowledge, spirituality, land protocols

TRADITIONAL SONGS 5
Inuit
My Breath/Orpingalik 5
Magic Words/Aua 8
Magic Words/Nakasuk 9
Song of the Girl Who Was Turning
 into Stone/Ivaluardjuk 9
Dead Man's Song/Netsit 10
Themes: orality, traditional knowledge, spirituality, land, language, protocols

JOSEPH BRANT 12
Mohawk
Letter 13
Condolence Speech 14
Themes: land, colonization, orality, treaty, sovereignty/nationhood

GEORGE COPWAY 15
Mississauga Ojibwe
A Word to the Reader 16
The Life of Kah-Ge-Ga-Gah-Bowh 16
Themes: autobiography, traditional knowledge, family/community, land

**CATHERINE SONEEGOH
 SUTTON** 24
Mississauga Ojibwe
Letter 24
Themes: land, history, colonization, gender, education

GHANDL 26
Haida
In His Father's Village, Someone
 Was Just About to Go Out
 Hunting Birds 26
Themes: orality, traditional knowledge/teachings, spirituality, land

E. PAULINE JOHNSON 36
Mohawk
A Cry from an Indian Wife 37
Shadow River 39
The Song My Paddle Sings 40
The Cattle Thief 41
The Corn Husker 43
Canadian Born 44
Themes: land, history, colonization, gender, aesthetics/language

MARY AUGUSTA TAPPAGE 44
Shuswap
Tyee—Big Chief 45
The Lillooets 45
Christmas at the Mission 46
At Birth 47
Themes: traditional knowledge/teachings, orality, community, Christianity

MARTIN MARTIN 48
Inuit
We, the Inuit, Are Changing 49
Themes: orality, colonialism, Christianity, traditional knowledge, community

ALMA GREENE 51
Mohawk
From *Forbidden Voice: Reflections of a Mohawk Indian* 51
Themes: treaty, land, voice, colonization, Christianity, gender

HARRY ROBINSON 56
Okanagan
Coyote Challenges God 57
A Woman Receives Power from a Deer 61
Themes: orality, traditional knowledge/teachings, spirituality, Christianity

MARION TUU'LUQ 67
Inuit
A Story of Starvation 67
Themes: orality, land, traditional knowledge, community, history

ARTHUR (ART) SOLOMON 71
Ojibwe Anishinaabe
Prisons Are an Abomination 72
Education 73
Spirit Helpers 74
On Native Spirituality 75
Opening the Bird Cages 77
Themes: incarceration, colonization, spirituality, education, freedom, trauma

HOWARD ADAMS 78
Métis
The Basis of Racism 79
Themes: colonialism/racism, history, identity, community, urbanization

GEORGE BLONDIN 84
Dene
My Own Medicine Story 85
What Is Medicine Power? 87
Themes: orality, land, traditional knowledge/teachings, spirituality

ALEXANDER WOLFE 88
Saulteaux Anishinaabe
The Last Grass Dance 89
Themes: orality, land, community, traditional knowledge, spirituality

BASIL H. JOHNSTON 93
Ojibwe Anishinaabe
The Prophecy 94
One Generation from Extinction 96
Is That All There Is? Tribal Literature 101
Birds 109
Themes: Indigenous language, history, traditional knowledge, spirituality

RITA JOE 112
Mi'kmaw
Today's Learning Child 113
I Lost My Talk 114
Micmac Hieroglyphics 114
Shanawdithit 115
The Lament of Donald Marshall Jr. 116

Learning the Language 117
Justice 117
When I am gone 118
Themes: *Indigenous voice/ language, history, aesthetics, education*

LOUIS BIRD 119
Omushkego (Swampy Cree)
Wihtigo Or, The Consequences of Not Listening 119
Conversions to Christianity 121
Themes: *orality, land, community, traditional teachings, spirituality*

DUKE REDBIRD 123
Chippewa Anishinaabe
The Beaver 124
My Moccasins 125
The Power of the Land 126
Themes: *land, community, traditional teachings, protest, aesthetics*

MARIA CAMPBELL 127
Métis
Good Dog Bob 128
Jacob 130
Themes: *humour, storytelling, Métis dialect, family, women*

BETH BRANT 138
Mohawk
Coyote Learns a New Trick 139
Swimming Upstream 141
Themes: *gender, sexuality, traditional knowledge, colonization*

BUFFY SAINTE-MARIE 146
Cree
Universal Soldier 147
Now That the Buffalo's Gone 148
My Country 'Tis of Thy People You're Dying 149
The War Racket 151
Themes: *protest, land, colonization, history, community, US politics*

ANNHARTE 152
Saulteaux Anishinaabe
Raced Out to Write This Up 152
Coyote Trail 154
Coyote Columbus Café 155
Got Something in the Eye 160
Exercises in Lip Pointing 161
How to Write About White People 164
Saskatchewan Indians Were Dancing 165
I Shoulda Said Something Political 165
Themes: *urban experience, gender, protest, colonization, humour, aesthetics*

THOMAS KING 168
Cherokee
The One About Coyote Going West 169
A Short History of Indians in Canada 176
'You'll Never Believe What Happened': The Truth About Stories 178
Themes: *storytelling, history, stereotypes, identity, humour*

HAROLD CARDINAL 182
Cree
A Canadian *What the Hell It's All About* 183
Themes: *Canadian politics, sovereignty/ nationhood, land, colonialism*

WAYNE KEON   190
Nipissing Anishinaabe
heritage   190
howlin at the moon   191
for donald marshall   192
i'm not in charge of this ritual   194
if i ever heard   195
my sweet maize   196
the apocalypse will begin   198
replanting the heritage tree   199
Themes: aesthetics/ language, history, colonialism, stereotypes, politics

BRIAN MARACLE   200
Kanyen'kehaka (Mohawk)
The First Words   201
Themes: spirituality, orality/ storytelling, traditional knowledge, protocols

JEANNETTE C. ARMSTRONG   212
Okanagan
History Lesson   213
The Disempowerment of First North American Native Peoples and Empowerment Through Their Writing   215
For Tony   218
Indian Woman   219
Threads of Old Memory   221
Wind Woman   224
Keepers Words   225
Themes: aesthetics, Indigenous language/writing, politics, traditional knowledge

MICHAEL ARVAARLUK KUSUGAK   227
Inuit
Kaugiagjuk   227
Themes: The North, traditional knowledge, myth, colonization

SHIRLEY STERLING   231
Nlaka'pamux (Interior Salish)
From *My Name is Seepeetza*   232
Themes: residential school, gender, language

LENORE KEESHIG   236
Ojibwe Anishinaabe
After Oka—How Has Canada Changed?   237
Indians   238
A Found Poem   238
Dance   240
O Canada (bear viii)   240
The White Man's Burden   241
Themes: aesthetics, politics, appropriation, stereotypes, colonization, land

EMMA LAROCQUE   246
Cree/Métis
A Personal Essay on Poverty   247
Themes: poverty, storytelling, family, urban experience

BEATRICE MOSIONIER   249
Métis
From *April Raintree*   249
Themes: urban experience, foster care, gender, murdered and missing

RITA BOUVIER   261
Métis
when hope is lost   262
sometimes I find myself weeping at the oddest moment   264
papîyâhtak   265
winter is certain   266
a ritual for goodbye   267
Themes: tradition, colonization, gender, ceremony, language, trauma

Contents | vii

LEE MARACLE 268
Métis/Salish
Yin Chin 269
Charlie 273
Blessing Song 279
Themes: residential school, ceremony, women, empowerment, land

TOMSON HIGHWAY 280
Cree
From *The Rez Sisters* 281
Why Cree Is the Funniest of All Languages 286
Themes: Language, humour, community, women, trauma, sexuality

ALOOTOOK IPELLIE 292
Inuit
Waking Up 293
Journey Toward Possibilities 296
Walking Both Sides of an Invisible Border 299
Summit with Sedna, the Mother of Sea Beasts 301
Themes: aesthetics/writing, traditional knowledge, colonialism, land, urbanization

MARGO KANE 304
Saulteaux/Cree
From *Moonlodge* 305
Themes: women, ceremony, tradition, residential school, theatre

DUNCAN MERCREDI 316
Inninew/Cree
could be anyone but i call him syd 317
statue 318
god shrugged and turned his back 319
big bear 320
kiskisin (i remember) 321
Themes: urban experience, language, history, aesthetics

DANIEL DAVID MOSES 323
Delaware
Report on Anna Mae's Remains 323
The Persistence of Songs 324
Some Grand River Blues 325
Inukshuk 326
Hotel Centrale, Rotterdam 328
Cry, a chorale, a work for theatre 329
My Discovery of America 332
Themes: aesthetics, colonization, land, urbanization, politics

RUBY SLIPPERJACK 333
Ojibwe Anishinaabe
Blueberry Days 334
Themes: land, identity, traditional knowledge, community, storytelling

LOUISE HALFE 341
Cree
Pāhkahkos 341
She Told Me 343
Body Politics 344
Fog Inside Mama 345
Stones 346
My Ledders 348
The Heat of My Grandmothers 349
Residential School Alumni 350
maskwa—bear 351
ospwākan—the pipe 351
Burning in this Midnight Dream 352
Themes: aesthetics, humour, residential school, trauma, women, violence

SHARRON PROULX-TURNER 353
Métis
a horse's nest egg is very large 353
The house that's idle no more 359
Themes: trauma, violence, women, colonization, tradition

viii | Contents

MONIQUE MOJICA   361
Kuna/Rappahannock
From *Princess Pocahontas and the Blue Spots*   362
Themes: history, politics, aesthetics, humour, women, theatre

GARRY GOTTFRIEDSON   369
Secwepemc (Shuswap)
Whiskey Bullets   370
Sun Peak Lies   370
Winter Horses   371
Deaf Heaven   371
The Highway of Tears   372
Micromanagers   373
Secwepemcu'llucw   374
Themes: politics, colonization, masculinity, land, violence

MARILYN DUMONT   374
Cree/Métis
Squaw Poems   375
Let the Ponies Out   377
Horse-Fly Blue   377
Circle the Wagons   378
monuments, cowboys & indians, tin cans, and red wagons   379
the dimness of mothers and daughters   380
jig dream   381
Broadway   381
scorching   381
Otipemisiwak   383
Ode to the Red River Cart   384
Fiddle bids us   385
Louis' Last Vision   386
Themes: history, colonization, women, politics, land

MARVIN FRANCIS   387
Cree
mcPemmican™   387

PULLING FACES   389
BNA ACTOR   390
word drummers   392
Soup for the Hood   393
Themes: urban experience, history, colonization, aesthetics, racism

ARMAND GARNET RUFFO   394
Ojibwe Anishinaabe
Poem for Duncan Campbell Scott   395
From *Grey Owl: The Mystery of Archie Belaney*   396
Rockin' Chair Lady   399
In the Sierra Blanca   400
Sacred Bear from Vision, 1959–60   402
Indian Canoe   404
On the Day the World Begins Again   405
Themes: history, treaty, stereotypes, spirituality, aesthetics, incarceration

RICHARD WAGAMESE   406
Ojibwe Anishinaabe
Returning to Harmony   407
From *Indian Horse*   411
Themes: residential school, reconciliation, spirituality

ROBERT ARTHUR ALEXIE   417
Teetl'it Gwich'in
From *Porcupines and China Dolls*   418
Themes: community, residential school, violence, trauma, the North

PAUL SEESEQUASIS   427
Cree
The Republic of Tricksterism   428
Themes: aesthetics, traditional knowledge, politics, autobiography

JOANNE ARNOTT 434
Métis

Wiles of Girlhood 434
If Honour is Truth 436
Steepy Mountains 437
Dog Girl Verse 440
when you 441
Constance 443
Sah kee too win
  (elder's voice) 444
Themes: women, trauma, colonization, relationships, aesthetics

CONNIE FIFE 444
Cree

Dream 445
Driftwoodwoman 446
the knowing 446
speaking through
  jagged rock 448
poem for Russell 448
For Matthew Shepard 449
Exiled 450
Witnessing 450
Edmonton to Regina 451
Themes: politics, land, relationships, women

DREW HAYDEN TAYLOR 452
Ojibwe Anishinaabe

Pretty Like a White Boy: The
  Adventures of a Blue-Eyed
  Ojibway 453
Someday 456
Themes: the reserve, urbanization, stereotypes, humour, theatre

MARIE CLEMENTS 463
Métis

From *Urban Tattoo* 464
Themes: theatre, urban experience, land, women, myth, trauma

JANET ROGERS 473
Mohawk/ Tuscarora

What the Carver Knows 474
Giving A S**T, An Idle No More
  Poem 475
Human Rights 478
Reading Cards 480
No More Birthdays 482
Themes: identity, women, history, colonization, empowerment, Idle No More

JOSEPH A. DANDURAND 483
Kwantlen

drunks, drifters and fat robins 484
St Mary's I 485
perfection 487
nice day 488
My confession 489
Living hell 491
We walk together 492
Themes: community, the reserve, land, politics, poverty, residential school

KATERI AKIWENZIE-DAMM 494
Ojibwe Anishinaabe

kegedonce 495
Grandmother, Grandfather 496
The Stone Eater 496
Themes: community, relationships, women, colonization, family

GREGORY SCOFIELD 499
Métis

Nothing Sacred 500
Âyahkwêw's Lodge 501
Promises 502
Cycle (of the Black Lizard) 502
Warrior Mask 504
Ôchîm ♦ His Kiss 505
Hunger 506

My Drum His Hands   507
Wâstêpakâwi-pîsim   508
Night Train   509
This Is My Blanket   510
The Infinity of Maybe   511
Dear Sir to You I Say   512
Ghost Dance   513
Poem for the Group of Seven   514
Themes: politics, aesthetics, relationships, language, colonization, two spirit

RANDY LUNDY   516
Cree
Geography   516
Heal   517
Old Man & Old Woman in the Garden   518
Migrations   519
She   519
Dawn   520
The Gift of the Hawk   520
Bear   521
Cypress Hills   521
Surrender   522
Themes: land, relationships, traditional, knowledge

EDEN ROBINSON   523
Haisla/Heiltsuk
Terminal Avenue   523
From *The Sasquatch At Home*   529
Themes: land, violence, myth, spirituality, urbanization

DAVID A. GROULX   531
Ojibwe Anishinaabe
In the Cold October Waters   532
My Neighbour   532
One Swollen Afternoon   533
This Noise Is Life   533
Half-Breed Trek   534
Our House Was on a Dirt Road   534

Water   535
What Are Indians?   536
Themes: family, poverty, disempowerment, identity, violence, masculinity

PHILIP KEVIN PAUL   536
WSÀNEC' (Saanich)
The Cost   537
Taking the Names Down from the Hill   538
On Their Wedding Anniversary   540
Descent into Sannich   542
Released from an Ordinary Night   542
Perching   543
Themes: family, heredity, community, land, tradition, colonization

LEANNE BETASAMOSAKE SIMPSON   544
Michi Saagiig Anishinaabe
Want   545
leaks   546
lost in a world where he was always the only one   547
Leaning In   550
Themes: land, traditional knowledge, women, urban

RICHARD VAN CAMP   551
Dogrib
Mermaids   552
the uranium leaking from port radium and rayrock mines is killing us   560
Why Ravens Smile to Little Old Ladies as They Walk By . . .   561
Themes: the North, humour, land, community

ROSANNA DEERCHILD 563
Cree
how to hunt moose 564
worth 564
mama making moccasins 565
ceremony 566
on the first day 567
bread crumbs 568
when I think of Mama in
    Residential School 570
*Themes: the north, residential
    schools, women, violence, racism*

LISA BIRD-WILSON 571
Métis
blood memory 571
Themes: tradition, women, identity

TANYA TAGAQ 576
Inuit
From *Split Tooth* 576
*Themes: north, sexuality,
    colonization, residential school,
    violence, language*

CHERIE DIMALINE 579
Métis
The Marrow Thieves 580
*Themes: residential schools, youth,
    tradition*

TARA BEAGAN 590
Ntlaka'pamux
From *In Spirit* 590
*Themes: missing and murdered,
    violence, storytelling, aesthetics,
    theatre*

LESLEY BELLEAU 598
Ojibwe Anishinaabe
Silence Is Not Our Mother
    Tongue 599
This Is Indian Land 602
Sunday at the Healing Lodge 604
*Themes: ceremony, women,
    land, trauma, violence,
    'Idle No More'*

**DAVID ALEXANDER
ROBERTSON 605**
Swampy Cree
From *Betty: The Helen Betty
    Osborne Story* 606
*Themes: murdered and missing,
    urban, the north, graphic
    novel, history*

KATHERENA VERMETTE 619
Métis
mixed tape 619
indians 621
blue jay 622
family 623
where 624
bury me at Batoche 626
*Themes: urban, racism, youth,
    murdered and missing, history*

DAWN DUMONT 627
Plains Cree
The Stars (February 2008) 628
*Themes: the reserve, urbanization,
    stereotypes, policing, power, violence*

WAUBGESHIG RICE 632
Ojibwe Anishinaabe
Dust 633
*Themes: the rez, politics, family,
    tradition*

shalan joudry 641
Mi'kmaw
Su'nl 641
Africa/Indigenous 642

That Leaving Night   643
Ceremony for You   644
(Untitled)   645
Themes: land, ceremony, love, spirituality, violence, empowerment

JORDAN ABEL   646
Nisga'a
From *The Place of Scraps*   646
From *Injun*   649
Themes: aesthetics, language, identity, history, community, stereotypes

LIZ HOWARD   652
Ojibwe Anishinaabe
Boreal Swing   652
Contact   653
Anarchaeology of Lichen   654
Knausgaard, Nova Scotia   655
Themes: aesthetics, identity, family, history, trauma, north

JOSHUA WHITEHEAD   657
Oji-Cree
Jonny Appleseed   658
Themes: the rez, myth, two spirit, youth, violence

BILLY-RAY BELCOURT   668
Cree
The Rez Sisters II   668
Notes from a Public Washroom   669
Sacred   670
Colonialism: A Love Story   670
OkCupid   671
God Must Be an Indian   672
Love Is a Moontime Teaching   673
Themes: urban, two spirit, racism, colonization, tradition

Acknowledgements   674
Table of Contents by Genre   680
Index   686

A Timeline of Indigenous Literatures

Since Time Immemorial—A vast and diverse body of story, poetry, drama, and song representing every Indigenous nation on Turtle Island, now North America.

1700s—Treaties recorded in 'Indian Treaties and Surrender' documents created by colonial government representatives; the Indigenous perspective in these meetings is absent, indicating that the full record of negotiations is not documented.

1752—Indigenous leaders such as Chief Atecouando (Abenaki) react to settlement of Indigenous lands by colonists. Atecouando's speech demanding Captain Phineas Stevens, representing the governor of Boston, to stop breaking their treaty is recorded in New France.

1800s—Speeches by Chiefs are recorded and translated; they respond with anger and trepidation to the influx of settlers and to the treaties they are pressured to sign with the Crown.

1800s—Mohawk Joseph Brant—war chief, leader, treaty negotiator, diplomat and interpreter fluent in English and the Six Nations languages—writes to the British crown concerning land.

1847—Mississauga-Ojibwe George Copway publishes his memoir *The Life, History, and Travels of Kah-ge-ga-gah-bowh*.

1860—*Life and Journals of Kah-ke-wa-quo-na-by* by Mississauga-Ojibwe Reverend Peter Jones, Kahkewaquonaby, is published posthumously; a year later, his *History of the Ojebway Indians; With Especial Reference to Christianity* is published.

1884—An amendment to the Indian Act makes attendance at day schools or residential schools compulsory for First Nations children. The Canadian government develops a policy of 'aggressive assimilation'.

1800s—Métis leader and founder of the province of Manitoba, Louis Riel, writes poetry in French up until the time of his execution in 1885.

1894—*Legends of the MicMacs*, two volumes of narratives are collected, translated and published by Rev. Silas Tertius Rand; his Indigenous informants are not credited.

1895—Mohawk poet E. Pauline Johnson publishes *The White Wampum*; she travels widely performing her poetry to large, receptive audiences.

1900—Haida poet-storytellers, including Gandl and Skaay, are recorded by American anthropologist John Reed Swanton and translated with Haida interpreter Henry Moody. Their stories and poems are reinterpreted by Canadian poet Robert Bringhurst and published in three volumes, in 1999, 2001, and 2003 respectively.

1902–03—Métis military leader Gabriel Dumont (1837–1906) gives a detailed account of his life in the French-Michif dialect; in 1993 the account is translated into English by Michael Barnholden and published as *Gabriel Dumont Speaks*.

1903— E. Pauline Johnson publishes *Canadian Born*, revealing her patriotism to Canada and the complexity of her identity.

1910—Division of Anthropology within the Geological Survey of Canada is established and recruits anthropologists such as Franz Boas, Edward Sapir, Marius Barbeau, and Diamond Jenness to document and collect material and non-material Indigenous culture. Indigenous collaborators, such as Tlingit linguist George Hunt, assist these and other anthropologists.

1911—Stó:lo Chief William Sepass, K'HHalserten in the Halkomelm language, is credited as one of the first Indigenous authors in British Columbia. His stories and songs are transcribed and translated by Sophia White Street until 1915, and his work is posthumously published into the 2000s.

1912—Living in Vancouver, E. Pauline Johnson publishes *Flint and Feather*, the largest collection of her poems to appear in her lifetime; she dies in 1913.

1912—*Thirty Indian Legends of Canada* is published by Canadian writer and educator Margaret Bemister; she gives credit to one identifiable Indigenous informant, 'Okanagan chief Antowyne'.

1913—Superintendent of Indian Affairs Duncan Campbell Scott refuses to adequately fund residential schools and students suffer and die at 'alarming rates'. Education is secondary to manual labour and those who survive often leave the schools unable to read and write.

1918—*Canadian Wonder Tales* is published by John Lane, then reprinted in 1967 as *Glooskap's Country and Other Tales* by Cyrus MacMillan; no Indigenous informants are credited.

1920—School attendance at day or residential schools for all Indigenous children from seven to fifteen years old becomes obligatory. Creativity is all but stifled for generations.

1925—Linguist and professor at Yale University, Leonard Bloomfield, travels to Saskatchewan and records and translates Cree Elders. He publishes two collections from his recordings, *Sacred Stories of the Sweet Grass Cree* (1930) and *Plains Cree Texts* (1934).

1930s—Mohawk writer Dawendine (Bernice Loft Winslow) models herself after Pauline Johnston and tours until her marriage in 1937; *Iroquois Fires*, a collection of her 'lyrics and lore' is published in 1995.

1937—Traditional stories told by Cree Elder Adam Ballantyne from Pelican Narrows in northern Saskatchewan are recorded by geologist and teacher Prentice Downes and published in 1943 and 1949. Some are illustrated and republished in 1987 and into the 90s with credit given to Ballantyne, indicating the recognition and revitalization of the Indigenous storytelling tradition.

1940—Anahareo (Gertrude Bernard), a Mohawk from Mattawa, Ontario, publishes *My Life with Grey Owl*, after marrying the 'Indian imposter' Grey Owl (Archibald Belaney) in 1925; she rewrites and publishes it in 1972 as *Devil in Deerskins: My Life with Grey Owl*.

1955—*Totem, Tipi and Tumpline: Stories of Canadian Indians* by Olive M. Fisher and Clara L. Tyner is published, illustrating that much of the information at the time about First Nations is generalized and incorrect; the source texts are credited without informants.

1960—*Indian Legends of Canada* published by Ella Elizabeth Clark receives wide distribution; she acknowledges the 'Indians of Alberta'; no specific Indigenous informants are credited.

1963—*Tales of Nanabozho* wins of the 'Book-of-the-Year Award'; the collection is edited by Dorothy M. Reid, who credits nineteenth-century American ethnologist Henry R. Schoolcraft; we know today that much of Schoolcraft's material came from Bamewawagezhikaquay (Jane Johnston), his Ojibwe wife.

1965—*Legends of My People: The Great Ojibway*, 'illustrated and told' by the Ojibwe painter Norval Morrisseau, is published; artist and educator Selwyn Dewdney is credited as editor.

1967—Chief Dan George—actor, writer, and Indigenous rights advocate of the Tsleil-Waututh Nation—recites his poem 'A Lament for Confederation' at Vancouver's celebration for Canada's centennial.

1967—George Clutesi, Tseshaht artist, actor, and writer, publishes *Son of Raven, Son of Deer*, a series of reinterpreted traditional narratives with illustrations by Clutesi; it is followed by his long, illustrated narrative *Potlatch* in 1969, a forerunner to the contemporary Indigenous graphic novel.

1969—Harold Cardinal publishes *The Unjust Society* in response to the Trudeau government's 'White Paper'.

1969—*I Am an Indian*, compiled by Canadian editor Ken Gooderham, becomes the first anthology of writing by Indigenous authors to be published in Canada.

1970—Waubageshig (Harvey McCue) edits *The Only Good Indian: Essays by Canadian Indians*; it addresses topical issues of the day, such as education, that still resonate today.

1970—*Trapping Is My Life* by Slavey trapper John Tetso is published along with many other memoirs during this period, including *An Indian Remembers* by Tom Boulanger, 1971; *Chiefly Indian* by Henry Pennier, 1972; *The Days of Augusta* by Mary Augusta Tappage, 1973.

1971—*Sacred Legends of the Sandy Lake Cree* is published by Cree artist Carl Ray and James Stevens; the first edition credits Ray only with the illustrations; later editions correct this oversight.

1971—Potawatomi-Odawa artist Daphne Odjig publishes her ten-book Nanabush series, which is adopted by the Manitoba Department of Education. Like the work of Morrisseau, Clutesi, and Ray, it is an early example of an Indigenous artist combining story and graphic art.

1971—*Red on White: The Biography of Duke Redbird*, an experimental text employing concrete poetry, is published by Marty Dunn and Duke Redbird.

1972—The Association for Development in the Performing and Visual Arts (ANDPVA) is established by James Buller in Toronto.

1973—Maria Campbell's *Halfbreed* brings national attention to the plight of Indigenous women.

1973—*Geniesh: An Indian Girlhood*, by Jane Willis, becomes the first Indigenous book in Canada to give a personal account of residential school.

1975—Lee Maracle records and writes her memoir *Bobbi Lee: Indian Rebel*. Maracle's name is absent from the cover; an expanded edition in 1990 credits her as the author.

1977—*Many Voices: An Anthology of Contemporary Canadian Indian Poetry* is published by Canadian poets Marilyn Bowering and David Day; it includes non-Indigenous poets writing about Indigenous themes.

1977—*My Stories Are My Wealth* by Yukon Elders Angela Sidney, Kitty Smith, and Rachel Dawson, collected by anthropologist Julie Cruikshank, is published by The Council for Yukon Indians. This community-based text becomes an example for other communities collecting and preserving their traditional stories. Cruikshank will go on to collaborate with Athapaskan and Tlingit Elders to produce the award-winning *Life Lived Like a Story* (1991).

1978—Mini Aodla Freeman's *Life Among the Qallunaat* is nominated for a Governor General's Award for Non-fiction. The 1970s saw Inuit literature in Canada begin to reach a wider audience with such publications as Markoosie's *Harpoon of the Hunter* (1974) and Anthony Trasher's *Trasher: Skid Row Eskimo* (1978).

1979—*Shuswap Stories*, collected by Randy Bouchard and Dorothy Kennedy, is published. Credit is given to Shuswap storytellers Isaac Willard, Nellie Thomas, Aimee August, and Charley Draney; August and Draney are also credited with translation. Accreditation will become the norm into the 1980s.

1979—The En'owkin (educational and cultural) Centre is founded in Penticton, BC, and begins to train Indigenous writers.

1980—Pemmican Publications is incorporated in Winnipeg by the Manitoba Métis Federation and considered the first Indigenous trade publisher in Canada.

1981—Theytus Books is incorporated as an independent Indigenous publisher by Randy Fred. Nurturing new talent, it becomes a leading Indigenous publisher.

1982—Native Earth Performing Arts (theatre company) is established in Toronto and becomes a 'hotbed' of creativity; playwrights begin to examine the mythic roots of Indigenous storytelling.

1983—Beatrice Mosionier (formally Culleton) publishes *In Search of April Raintree*, now recognized as the first novel written by an Indigenous writer in Canada.

1985—Jeannette C. Armstrong's political novel *Slash* is published through Theytus Books.

1986—Tomson Highway's *The Rez Sisters* premieres and becomes a mega success; it wins the Dora Mavor Moore Award for Outstanding New Play and ushers in contemporary Indigenous theatre, while bringing attention to Indigenous creative writing in general.

1988—Lee Maracle publishes *I Am Woman: A Native Perspective on Sociology and Feminism*, written 'to empower Native women'.

1989—*Seventh Generation: Contemporary Native Writing*, published by Theytus Books, is the first anthology of contemporary Indigenous poets.

1990—Theytus Books begins publishing *Gatherings: The En'owkin Journal of First North American Peoples*, giving a vehicle for emerging Indigenous writers to publish in.

1990—Thomas King's *Medicine River* is published by Viking Canada, part of the Penguin Group, bringing international attention to Indigenous literature in Canada; it is adapted to a television movie and viewed nationally.

1990—*Native Literature in Canada: From the Oral Tradition to the Present*, the first historical overview of Indigenous literature in Canada, is published by Dr. Penny Petrone.

1990—The Oka Crisis over disputed Mohawk land inspires responses from Indigenous writers nationally.

1990—The academic journal *Canadian Literature* publishes its special issue 'Native Writers and Canadian Literature', bringing Indigenous writing to the Canadian literary establishment.

1990—*All My Relations*, edited by Thomas King, published by McClelland and Steward, is the first collection of Indigenous short stories by a major Canadian publisher.

1990—*Writing the Circle: Native Women of Western Canada* is the first collection of Indigenous women's creative writing; Cree-Métis scholar Emma LaRocque writes an important critical introduction.

1990—Kanyen'kehà:ka (Mohawk) resistance, known as 'The Oka Crisis,' over disputed Mohawk land inspires responses from Indigenous writers nationally.

1991—The Royal Commission on Aboriginal Peoples is established. The final report of 4,000 pages, overseen by both Indigenous and non-Indigenous commissioners, is critical of Canada's ongoing colonial relationship to Indigenous peoples. It is shelved.

1992—Oxford University Press publishes the first edition of *An Anthology of Canadian Native Literature in English*, bringing international attention to the literature.

1993—*Looking at the Words of Our People*, edited by Jeannette C. Armstrong, becomes the first book of Indigenous literary criticism in Canada.

1993—The 'Indigenous Arts Program' is formally established at the Banff Centre for Arts and Creativity in Banff, Alberta.

1994—The 'Writing Thru Race' conference is held in Vancouver to address the 'appropriation of voice' issue; it creates division in the Writers Union of Canada.

1994—Cree poet Louise Halfe publishes *Bear Bones and Feathers* and wins the Pat Lowther First Book Award and the Gerald Lampert Award; her writing mixes English and Cree language and shows creative possibilities for Indigenous writers.

1994—Ojibwe writer Richard Wagamese publishes his comedic novel *Keeper'n Me*, revealing the traumatic intergenerational impact of the residential school system.

1994—Playwright Tomson Highway is made a member of the Order of Canada.

1995—The 'Aboriginal Women's Voices' program is established at the Banff Centre for the Arts and Creativity in Banff, Alberta.

1995—The 'Ipperwash Crisis' over disputed Indigenous land in Ipperwash Provincial Park in Ontario inspires Indigenous writers.

1996—The last residential school operated by the Canadian government, the Gordon Indian Residential School in Saskatchewan, closes.

1996—Marilyn Dumont publishes the poetry collection *A Really Good Brown Girl*; she wins the Gerald Lambert Award and brings national attention to contemporary Métis writing.

1997—Métis writer Ian Ross becomes the first Indigenous playwright to win the Governor General's Literary Award for Drama, for *fareWel*.

1997—Métis poet Gregory Scofield publishes *Love Medicine and One Song*, opening a door for eroticism in Indigenous writing.

1999—The MacKenzie Art Gallery publishes *Exposed: Aesthetics of Aboriginal Erotic Art* and includes erotic poetry by Indigenous poets.

2000—'ImagineNATIVE film + Media Arts Festival' is founded in Toronto to support the work of Indigenous directors, producers, and screenwriters.

2001—Artist-writer Michael Nicoll Yahgulanaas publishes *A Tale of Two Shamans*, considered one of the very first Indigenous graphic novels published in Canada; in 2009 he publishes his highly successful *Red, A Haida Manga*. Graphic novels become a popular form of Indigenous literary expression.

2003—Thomas King becomes the first Indigenous writer to give the 'CBC Massey Lectures'; he gives his talk on 'The Truth About Stories'.

2004—'For the Love of Words: Aboriginal Writers of Canada' conference is organized at the University of Manitoba; it brings together for the first time Indigenous writers and scholars working in the field of Indigenous literature.

2005—The 'Indigenous Writing Program' is established at the Banff Centre for Arts and Creativity in Banff, Alberta. Numerous Indigenous writers go through the program.

2006—Anishinaabe artist and writer Leo Yerxa wins the Governor General's Literary Award for his illustrated children's book *Ancient Thunder*.

2007—The 'Brandon Aboriginal Literary Festival', hosted by Brandon University, brings together for the first time 25 established and emerging Indigenous writers.

2007—Truth and Reconciliation Commission on Indian Residential Schools is initiated; it runs until 2015 and produces a report consisting of 94 'Calls to Action.' Indigenous writers respond to the horrors of the testimony.

2008—'The Centre for Creative Writing and Oral Culture', the first institute of its kind in Canada, is founded at the University of Manitoba.

2008—The Canada Council for the Arts establishes an 'Aboriginal Arts Office'.

2012—The 'Idle No More' movement begins with four women and spreads across the country; two years later *The Winter We Danced* is published, an anthology of 'Voices from the Past, the Future and the Idle No More Movement'.

2012—The Burt Award for First Nations, Métis and Inuit Literature is established by the Canadian Organization for Development through Education (CODE) and presented annually for the best works of young adult literature in Canada.

2013—Richard Wagamese wins the inaugural Burt Award for his novel *Indian Horse*.

2013—The Indigenous Literary Studies Association (ILSA) is created to focus specifically on the study and teaching of Indigenous peoples' literatures.

2013—Métis writer Katherena Vermette becomes the first Indigenous poet to win the Governor General's Literary Award for *North End Love Songs*.

2013—*Two-Spirit Acts, Queer Indigenous Performances* is published; Tomson Highway writes the foreword.

2014—Ojibwe poet Armand Garnet Ruffo is invited to teach poetry for 'Literature Wales' at the Tŷ Newydd Writing Centre in Criccieth, Wales, indicating that Indigenous poets are now being read internationally.

2014—Thomas King becomes the first Indigenous writer to win the Governor General's Literary Award for Fiction, for *The Back of the Turtle,* and the first Indigenous writer to be awarded the RBC Taylor Prize for literary non-fiction for *The Inconvenient Indian: A Curious Account of Native People.*

2014—Queen's University in Kingston, Ontario, creates the academic position of a 'Queen's National Scholar in Indigenous Literature', indicating that the field is now mainstream.

2015—Prolific author and Ojibwe language advocate Basil Johnston dies.

2016—Ojibwe poet Liz Howard becomes the first Indigenous poet to win the Griffin Poetry Prize for *Infinite Citizen of the Shaking Tent*. In subsequent years, two other young Indigenous poets, Jordan Abel (2017) and Billy-Ray Belcourt (2018), win the award.

2016—The Federal Government establishes the National Inquiry into Missing and Murdered Indigenous Women and Girls; writers respond.

2016—The appropriation of Indigenous identity and stories comes to a head with Canadian novelist Joseph Boyden; the appropriation issue is ongoing and was originally brought to the public's attention by poet Lenore Keeshig [Tobias] in a 1990 *Globe and Mail* article.

2017—Acclaimed novelist Richard Wagamese dies unexpectedly while working on his posthumously published novel, *Starlight*.

2017—The Indigenous Literary Studies Association (ILSA) establishes 'The Indigenous Voices Awards' (IVAs) for emerging writers, which 'aims to support Indigenous literary production in all its diversity and complexity'.

2017—Métis writer Cherie Dimaline wins the Governor General's Literary Award in the category of 'Young Peoples' Literature' for her novel *The Marrow Thieves*, which becomes hugely successful.

2018—Indigenous journalist Tanya Talaga wins the RBC Taylor Prize for literary non-fiction for *Seven Fallen Feathers: Racism, Death, and Hard Truths in a Northern City*. She gives the prestigious 'CBC Massey Lectures', focusing on the alarming rate of Indigenous youth suicide in colonized nations, published under the title *All Our Relations: Finding the Path Forward*.

2018—Playwrights Canada Press publishes *Indian Act: Residential School Plays*, illustrating that the broad range of residential school experiences has become a source of creativity and regeneration for Indigenous writers.

2018—Cree writer and former lands claim negotiator Darrel J. McLeod wins the Governor General's Literary Award in the category of non-fiction for *Mamaskatch: A Cree Coming of Age*, a memoir of an intergenerational residential school survivor.

2019—Greg Younging dies—Cree educator, activist, writer (of the *Indigenous Elements of Style: A Guide for Writing By and About Indigenous Peoples*, 2018) and long-time editor of Theytus Books.

2020—Indigenous writing continues to grow at an unprecedented rate; writers in all genres publish prolifically.

Preface to the Fifth Edition

As Armand mentions in his introductory essay, the field of Indigenous literature has indeed grown in leaps and bounds since the last edition, a mere six years ago. Today's CanLit seems to be much more inclusive to Indigenous writing, and as a result, the landscape for Indigenous writers has expanded and shifted in this place now called Canada. To me, this change is all about opportunity, not talent—there have always been exceptionally talented Indigenous writers—but now, we can also celebrate so many more published books, award wins and bestsellers, too. As we look ahead to the next six years and beyond, we can hope, perhaps a little more optimistically, that this long overdue recognition will continue.

With so much new writing over the last few years, our work putting this anthology together was exciting but very difficult. We had to make several tough decisions as we tried to include the very best Indigenous writing has to offer, as well as represent a wide array of genres and as many communities as possible. The result is this large volume you hold in your hands, but nevertheless, it is still only a portion of the larger story of Indigenous nations and artists working in literary forms. There are many writers we were not able to include, too many to mention here, but with hopes for their inclusion in later editions.

Our first selections were from writers already included in previous editions, and many of them, the vast majority of those still working, had produced new books, often more than one. As a result, we can happily include new writing from several of our formidable mid-career writers, such as Eden Robinson, Lee Maracle, and my fellow editor Armand Garnet Ruffo. We can even include new work from Maria Campbell and Buffy St Marie, as those two legends don't seem to tire at all.

Our next selection was from the veritable bumper crop of new writers who have produced work of immense value and craft since the last edition. As mentioned, we were only able to include a portion, but it is an extraordinary portion, and we were able to include over a dozen new writers here. These are names you have undoubtedly heard of, such as David Robertson, Cherie Dimaline, and Waubegeshig Rice. As well, we could not ignore the exceptional debuts of new writers, Tanya Tagaq, Joshua Whitehead, and Billy-Ray Bellcourt.

In the end, this anthology is filled with the strength and love of these artists, and our immense gratitude for their work. For me, this anthology represents the vast Indigenous literary traditions and trailblazers that have inspired and lead us here. It is because of the diligence, perseverance, and often sacrifice of those who have come before us that we are able to work today. This book also represents the future, as we excitedly anticipate new work from existing writers, and proudly admire the rise of many more new, young voices coming to the forefront in this opportune time.

Richard Van Camp has called this 'the Golden Age' of Indigenous Literature in this place now called Canada. I do agree that we are truly in a gilded time, but if

'Golden' means apex, then I have to respectfully disagree with one of my favourite mentors: I don't think we're at the peak yet. On the contrary, I think we're just getting started.

In solidarity,
Katherena Vermette
Winnipeg, Manitoba

Introduction

Armand Garnet Ruffo

Since the first edition of *An Anthology of Canadian Native Literature in English* in 1992 there have been unprecedented developments in the field of Indigenous literature in Canada. To say that the field has grown by leaps and bounds would not be an overstatement. This anthology alone has now gone through four editions, each featuring new authors and new work from previously published authors. As a way of introducing the first anthology, my former co-editors, Daniel David Moses and Terry Goldie, chose to dialogue between themselves, joining a conversation about the literature that continues to this day. For the fourth edition, they asked me to add my own voice by writing an overview of my experiences in the field, including the history of its development and the trends that I have seen. At the time I thought that it seemed fitting to start by recalling a job that I had with *The Native Perspective Magazine* in 1978. For this fifth incarnation of the anthology, I still see its relevance in providing some historical context to a body of literature that many readers coming to it for the first time undoubtedly take for granted.

In those days there was no such thing as Indigenous literature—at least not as it is understood today. Certainly, there was a substantial body of literature written since the beginning of the colonial period *about* Indigenous people, and even some texts written by Indigenous peoples themselves, and of course there was a whole body of translations from the oral tradition, but as a discursive field of study it did not exist. The whole field of Indigenous Studies was in its infancy, Indigenous literature in Canada not yet even on its radar, let alone having a separate space dedicated to it. As for post-colonial studies, Edward Said's groundbreaking *Orientalism*, coincidentally published in 1978, was hardly off the press, and it would take some time before minority literatures within the former colonies, such as Canada, were even considered. Canada's claim to be included within the 'post-colonial' would be therefore immediately challenged by Indigenous writers and scholars who would see this assertion as both ironic considering their marginalized status within the country and offensive because on the face of it the term 'post-colonial' implied an erasure of their pre-contact histories.

That summer, then, I found myself in Ottawa working for *The Native Perspective Magazine*, where the editor gave me a couple of assignments that coincided with my rather unusual—for the time—interest in Indigenous literature. First, I was asked to write a short biography on the Mohawk poet E. Pauline Johnson, about whom I had an inkling because of my Ojibwe grandmother's interest in poetry. I was also asked to start a 'literary corner', which would include writing from across the country. Because of the long silence due to the residential school period, which effectively halted the development of literary writing, Indigenous people were eager to see themselves in print and the magazine received a flurry of submissions of poetry, memoir, short fiction, traditional stories, and essays. Most of the contributors were what I have called elsewhere 'occasional writers'.[1] By this I mean those people who wrote only occasionally and were celebrating the 'occasion' of surviving assimilation and their pride and identity as Indigenous—though by no means was all the writing cheerful or positive in dealing with the loss, pain, anger, and resistance that is part and parcel of a heritage of colonialism. And while a few of the poets, writers, and storytellers—like Duke Redbird and Rita Joe—were getting published in small anthologies like Kent Gooderman's *I Am Indian* (1969) and David Day and Marilyn Bowering's *Many Voices: An Anthology of Contemporary Canadian Indian Poetry* (1977), and publishing their own books, Indigenous literature remained on the margins of literary Canada and was virtually non-existent in the eyes of the general public. Basil Johnston aptly describes this intolerable situation in his essay 'Is That All There Is? Tribal Literature', which recalls an incident in the early 1970s that got him interested in writing. He states matter-of-factly about that time: 'There is fortunately enough [Indigenous] literature, both oral and written, available for scholarly study, but it has for the most part been neglected.'[2] Although Canada's official adoption of multiculturalism in 1971 would help change the face of Canadian literature, the attitude still remained that only European cultures, preferably Anglo-Saxon or French, the official gaze and record of the time, could produce literature in Canada.

To understand why contemporary Indigenous writers began to assert themselves into the Canadian consciousness when they did, we have to step back and consider this 'coming to voice' in the context of the repercussions of colonialism. It is now understood that Indigenous peoples in what is now Canada have endured a history of dispossession (from language, culture, land, economic sustainability), forced relocation, and a steady campaign of propaganda that has preached a doctrine of assimilation to 'superior' English and French cultures. It also common knowledge that this onslaught by Euro-Canadians culminated in the legally sanctioned institution of the residential school, which saw generations of Indigenous children forcibly removed from their families and communities and cut off from their languages and traditions. In literary terms, one might think of it in this way: these schools effectively severed whatever influence Pauline Johnson might have had on the next generation of Indigenous writers. Unlike the preceding generations of the nineteenth century, and authors of those generations such as George Copway (and Louis Riel writing in French), who had attended seminaries or missionary schools and learned to write effectively, the following generations would not pick up the pen (effortlessly) because governmental residential schools were not established to educate Indigenous children in any meaningful way. In speaking of her own sister, Lee Maracle (Coastal Salish-Métis) has said that to compound the tragedy of the schools, the children were not even provided with any kind of real education; after spending years in residential school doing manual labour her sister left barely able to read and write. Of course, there are always exceptions to the rule, and it is survivors like Basil Johnston and Harold Cardinal who would be among the first generation after the residential school period to begin writing and publishing. Writing by residential school survivors Shirley Stirling and Louise Halfe provide insight into this experience, though it is safe to say that the long shadow of residential school colours much of the work in the anthology, as witnessed in the writing of Richard Wagamese.

While writing by Indigenous authors, then—such as Harold Cardinal, Maria Campbell, Basil Johnston, Rita Joe, and Duke Redbird—started to become more prominent in the 1970s, it wasn't until the late 1980s and early 1990s that contemporary Indigenous literature began to be taken seriously and to make inroads into the consciousness of literary Canada. We can now see that this literary resurgence or renaissance was the direct result of converging factors that had to do with the political and social landscape of the time. A previous generation had returned home from the Second World War and Korea only to find the same discrimination and poverty they had thought they had left behind. In search of a better life, many moved to cities from Halifax to Vancouver, where cultural and linguistic differences gave way to common socio-political concerns. Later generations, inspired by the Civil Rights movement that was sweeping across the United States in the 1960s, and no longer willing to let the Church and State control their lives, began to form effective political organizations and agitate at the grassroots level to push hard for social change. In response to Trudeau's 'White Paper' (1969),[3] for example, which proposed an end to Indian status in the interests of a 'just society', Cree writer and politician Harold Cardinal published *The Unjust Society* (1969) which speaks of the life of his people in the context of the government's proposal to dismiss 500 years of historical record. This text along with his follow up, *The Rebirth of Canada's Indians* (1977), were seminal to the decade and address the legacy of disempowerment of Indigenous peoples and the subsequent rebirth through socio-political action. Because of the tragedy of the residential schools, education became a priority for Indigenous peoples, and, in 1972, The National Indian Brotherhood released its position paper, 'Indian Control of Indian Education'. That same year Trent University in Peterborough established the first Department of Native Studies in Canada. Meanwhile writers and activists such as Basil Johnston, Jeannette Armstrong, and Art Solomon spoke of the disastrous effects of the state's assimilative policies on Indigenous language and culture as witnessed by the exceedingly high rates of Indigenous incarceration, foster care, and homelessness. Though the education of Indigenous peoples would continue to be seriously underfunded by both federal and provincial governments by the 1980s and 1990s, a new generation was now graduating from mainstream universities and colleges, or Indigenous-run educational institutions like the En'owkin Centre in British Columbia and the Gabriel Dumont Institute in Saskatchewan, and eager to use their skills to express pride in their culture and to press for change through their writing.

Furthermore, to write one does not need a huge amount of money, or even education for that matter (though it certainly helps); as Maria Campbell has notably said, 'all you need is a pencil and a piece of paper; it doesn't cost you much.'[4] Another important factor is the sense of community that was developing among the writers as they began to meet each other at various venues. This sense of solidarity provided mutual support among the writers and reinforced the idea that they were not alone but engaged in a movement larger than themselves and for the common good of their people. The literary breakthrough, then, coincided with Indigenous people continuing to push politically for autonomy and self-determination while, on the cultural front, concurrently editing and publishing their own work, as exemplified in the anthologies *Contemporary Native Writing: Seventh Generation*, edited by Heather Hodgson (1989) and *Gatherings: The En'owkin Journal of First North American Peoples,* Theytus Books' annual publication, first published in 1990. Collaborations were also taking place, most notably in Harry Robinson and Wendy Wickwire's *Write It On Your Heart* (1989) and Jeanne Perreault and Sylvia Vance's *Writing The Circle: Native Women of Western Canada* (1990), in which Métis scholar Emma LaRocque in her groundbreaking critical introduction to the field brought the literature into perspective by tying it to Indigenous resistance. It is through such publications that Indigenous storytellers and writers began to be heard—making academic institutions and the general public finally begin to take notice.

At this point it is worth mentioning that south of the border, writing by Native Americans had already achieved considerable prominence. In contrast to Indigenous authors in Canada, Native American writers had already begun to be recognized by the broader public and were winning major literary awards. In 1969 N. Scott Momaday (Kiowa) was awarded the prestigious Pulitzer Prize for his novel *House Made of Dawn* (1968), and it is this period and Momaday's texts, including *The Way to Rainy Mountain* (1969), that are said to mark the beginning of the 'Native American Renaissance'.[5] It is interesting to note the strikingly different publishing histories between the two countries that laid the groundwork for their respective literary movements. In Canada, for any number of reasons—including limited access to a good education, dispossession, poverty, isolation, a much smaller population—contemporary Indigenous writers could look to only a handful of published works for inspiration and guidance, while in contrast, Native Americans already had a significant body of writing and publishing. For example, Native American authors have been publishing traditional stories, autobiographies, and histories since the early nineteenth century (and religious tracts even earlier) in numbers much greater than in Canada, and by the mid-twentieth century were even publishing important works of fiction. One only has to consider Joseph Mathews's (Osage) novel *Sundown* published in 1934 and D'Arcy McNickle's (Salish) novel *The Surrounded* published in 1936. (Granted, in Canada Pauline Johnson published both poetry and short fiction at the turn of the last century but she was pretty much the lone voice of Indigenous literature for her time.) Finally, it is important to note that, in large part, contemporary Native American authors emerged from institutions of higher learning. Momaday himself holds a Ph.D. in American Literature and held a professorship at the University of California, Santa Barbara, while writing *House Made of Dawn*. In this regard it would not be inaccurate to say that by the 1970s the vast majority of Native American writers who were actively publishing, including major writers such as James Welch (Blackfoot), Vine Deloria Jr. (Sioux), Leslie Marmon Silko (Laguna Pueblo), Simon Ortiz (Acoma Pueblo), Joy Harjo (Creek), and Paula Gunn Allen (Laguna Pueblo), like many of their literary predecessors, were all formally trained at American universities. This was far from the case in Canada, where it would take another twenty-five years for Indigenous peoples to begin graduating from universities and colleges in substantial numbers.

In his preface to *All My Relations: An Anthology of Contemporary Canadian Native Fiction*, another anthology to appear in the early 1990s, Thomas King (Cherokee), himself a transplanted Native American scholar with a Ph.D. from the University of Utah, provides a context for non-Indigenous readers unfamiliar with Indigenous literature. He defines the growing body of writing by Indigenous authors by referring to their shared cultural sense of past and continuing relations to family, community, animals, and land in 'intricate webs of kinship', while at the same time suggesting a diversity of form and content that cannot and should not be easily categorized. In doing so, he presents the provisional definition that 'Native literature is literature produced by Natives', which he qualifies by adding that 'providing we resist the temptation of trying to define a Native'.[6] Today we may not be any closer to a definition of Indigenous literature, but, as King suggested, we are now beginning to see 'patterns' emerging in recurring themes and concerns that are unique to Indigenous peoples because they specifically refer to 'the Indigenous experience', and moreover a convergence of these experiences since colonization. Whatever definition we arrive at, it is clear that Indigenous literature serves to counteract the erasure of Indigenous identities and cultures through a process of affirmation, recovery, and discovery of culture through story and other forms of literary expression.

This takes me to our current anthology. I don't think I would be off the mark to say that the publication of the first edition of Oxford University Press's *An Anthology of Canadian Native Literature in Canada* in 1992 did much to legitimize Indigenous literature in the eyes of mainstream Canada. By this I mean that Oxford's reputation and clout, in terms of dissemination and publicity, made general readers and scholars sit up and take notice. This is not to say that to some extent the literature was not still marginalized, but only that the first edition of this anthology went a long way towards introducing it to a broader audience and opening it to academic study by providing an accessible, comprehensive text. When I say 'comprehensive', I am referring to a text that for the first time in Canada surveyed Indigenous literature historically, beginning with traditional 'orature', (the term used by the first co-editors in this anthology) and concluding with contemporary writers, who for the most part have published since the mid-1980s. In their first introductory dialogue, the editors pointed to the potential for dissemination, nationally and internationally, that a publisher like Oxford represents.

Although this current anthology is still largely organized chronologically (with a thematic guide), the writing itself is not and moves through time and space thematically and stylistically according to the individual author. Beginning with what we might call foundational literature, namely that repository of the oral tradition that stretches back to time immemorial, the anthology fittingly opens with a short selection of anonymous orature that provides an example of the cultural roots of Indigenous literature. Prior to contact, orature was the primary way in which Indigenous peoples guarded and passed on information about their world and their existence in it. These stories served particular functions and were spiritual-mythic or secular-historical in nature; they either spoke of a world outside of historical time, the world of the 'manitous',[7] or within it, the world of daily living—though this separation is not always absolute. This selection provides the reader with an inherently sacred world view in which humankind and the natural world are integrated into a relationship based on kinship. Although the origin of this tradition is essentially pre-contact, it has evolved since contact and often incorporates the presence of the colonizer. The influence of the oral tradition on all Indigenous cultures echoes throughout the anthology in the writing of contemporary authors, who draw on the traditions of the sacred and the secular, by retelling, reinterpreting, and/or re-imagining. Contemporary Indigenous orature takes many forms, including stories written down by recorders, such as the Haida stories reinterpreted by Robert Bringhurst; put into writing by Indigenous authors with collaborators, such as in the Okanagan stories by storyteller Harry Robinson and Wendy Wickwire; written down by Indigenous writers, such as Basil Johnston (Ojibwe), George Blondin (Dene), and Louis Bird (Cree); or drawing on the influence of the oral tradition to create something totally new and individual like the writing of Thomas King (Cherokee), Beth Brant (Mohawk), Annharte (Anishinaabe), and Tomson Highway (Cree) to name only a few storytellers, poets, and writers represented in this anthology.

A few pages into the anthology the reader encounters letters from Joseph Brant (Mohawk) and Catherine Soneegoh Sutton (Ojibwe) as well as an excerpt from George Copway's (Mississauga) autobiography, *The Life, History and Travels of Kah-Ge-Ga-Gah-Bowh*. The arrival of the settlers in the Americas brought change of unfathomable proportion and consequence, and Indigenous people suddenly found themselves forced to adopt a new method of communication to address the impact of colonialism: writing in the language of the colonizer. 'I beg to say a few words more on this subject, the movements of Gov. Simcoe in attempting to curtail our lands to one half of the River,'[8] writes Brant, emphasizing that the major issue of the day was the encroachment of settlers on Indigenous lands and the resultant dispossession and displacement of his people. Equally forceful is Catherine Soneegoh Sutton's letter to 'The Editor of the Leader [who] appears [sic] to think that every Indian reservation is a publick [sic] nuisance so I conclude that if he could have his will, he would have every band of Indians drove on to the baran [sic] waste of granite rocks north of Lakes huron and superior.'[9] Suddenly faced with grievances that were essentially secular in nature, the loss of traditions, land, and self-determination, as the above letters indicate, Indigenous people inadvertently began to create a new tradition of Indigenous literature founded in the letters, memoirs, histories, and tracts on religious and political topics that they found themselves forced to write.

One of the first collections of Indigenous literature in Canada, *First People, First Voices* (1983), compiled by Penny Petrone, reveals that autobiography was the preferred genre of Indigenous authors during the colonial period, in which the authors use the events of their own lives to highlight the issues of the day. Copway's autobiography is in fact the first full English text written by an Indigenous writer in what would become Canada. A Christian conversion narrative, it simultaneously provides insight into the magnitude of the physical and emotional upheaval endured by the Indigenous peoples of that period. Copway struggles with the language of Christian charity to protect what he calls the 'remnants of this aboriginal race'.[10] Examples of the autobiography as a dominant form of discourse are evident throughout the present anthology and move through space and time from one end of the country to another, from Copway until today. In modern times, the power and influence of this 'new tradition' is best exemplified by Maria Campbell's bestselling autobiography *Halfbreed* (1973). Published at a time when Canadians knew little about Indigenous peoples, it brought national attention to the plight of Métis people, particularly women, making readers aware of the racism, intolerance, and injustice so prevalent across the country. For the first time a reality all too well known by Indigenous peoples became known to the general population. A key focus of autobiographical writing is the trend of 'the dispelling of lies and the telling of what really happened'.[11] Indigenous authors, for example, have exposed and examined the disastrous effects of the residential school experience as it pertains to the loss of Indigenous languages. This ongoing issue is highlighted in Rita Joe's seminal poem 'I Lost My Talk'[12] and Basil Johnston's essays 'One Generation from Extinction' and 'Is That All There Is? Tribal Literature',[13] which as noted reveals the initial impetus for Johnston's long and distinguished literary career. In this regard, this anthology includes new work by Louise Halfe, who details her own residential experiences in 'maskwa – bear'[14] and Rosanna Deerchild, who details her mother's experiences in 'bread crumbs'.[15]

Whether employing memoir, essay, fiction, poetry, or drama, Indigenous authors have varied the form of their writing while striving to 'reinvent' the language of the colonizer to find their own voice. Consider Mary Augusta Tappage (Shuswap), writing in the early twentieth century in British Columbia, who dedicated a good part of her life to the preservation of her Indigenous language, and whose memoir uses poetry to capture the rhythm of her 'mother tongue'. Rita Joe (Mi'kmaq), likewise committed to the preservation of her Indigenous language, writes a conversational poetry that gently prods her non-Indigenous readers to make room for her people. In her essay 'After Oka—How Has Canada Changed', Lenore Keeshig (Ojibwe-Anishinaabe) begins with a communal voice echoing an earlier time: 'My people are the Saugeen Ojibway. Our earliest claim against the Crown dates back to the Treaty of 1836 when our people were forced to cede 1.5 million acres of the richest land in Upper Canada.'[16] Joanne Arnott (Métis) uses her own life experiences, such as the birth of her children, and the techniques of poetry to write powerfully about identity issues. Paul Seesequasis (Cree) turns the autobiography into something new, like the 'mixed-bloods'[17] he writes about, employing outlandish parody and humour. In contrast to pure memoir, some Indigenous people have felt compelled to tell their story in fiction. Salish writer and educator Shirley Stirling is one such example, whose acclaimed *My Name is Seepeetza* (1992) is based on the experiences of the author and her sisters and friends who attended Kamloops residential school in the 1950s. The first novel by an Indigenous writer, Beatrice Culleton's *In Search of April Raintree,* was published in 1983 and immediately broke new ground. Based on her own experiences of growing up in foster homes in or near Winnipeg, it was initially drafted in response to the suicide of her sister. It however moves beyond the personal and becomes a vehicle for re-imagining and exploring the issues surrounding Métis identity. Like Campbell's *Halfbreed,* it is still read today and studied widely in curricula across the country.

In the 1980s the rising concern for Indigenous autonomy and control led to the establishment of Pemmican Publications, the original publisher of *In Search of April Raintree*. Founded in Winnipeg in 1980, with a mandate to give Métis writers an outlet for their work, it has since gone on to publish Indigenous writers such as Duncan Mercredi. A year later Theytus Books incorporated in Penticton, British Columbia, with a focus on Okanagan writing but also with a mandate of inclusiveness. In 1985, it published Jeannette Armstrong's *Slash,* a novel that employs a male protagonist to examine the identity of the S'yilx or Okanagan People in Penticton and their relationship to the land and community. Written in the episodic style of orature, the novel examines not only the effects of colonialism but also an Indigenous perspective on the resistance to it. As though a door had been opened in the 1980s, the following decade saw other writers actively begin to document their lives and those of their peoples through fiction. Stó:lō writer Lee Maracle's writing career illustrates the struggles of Indigenous people coming to voice. Her memoir *Bobbi Lee Indian Rebel* was originally published in the early 1970s under the name of her editor, but a changing socio-political climate allowed her to assert herself as a writer, leading to *Sojourner's Truth and Other Stories* in 1990, a collection that includes 'Yin Chin', which draws on her own life to blur the line between fiction and non-fiction. Publishing with Theytus Books and small feminist presses, Maracle has subsequently become one of the most prolific Indigenous authors in Canada, publishing fiction, poetry, and essays. This period also saw the publication of Ojibwe novelist Ruby Slipperjack's *Honour the Sun* (1987) and *Silent Words* (1992), which use her own experiences of growing up in Northern Ontario to provide intimate portraits of the spirit of Anishinaabe culture. In contrast, Ojibwe journalist and novelist Richard Wagamese's bestselling novel *Keeper'n Me* (1994) describes growing up in foster homes and his search for his own Anishinaabe identity. It too mirrors his experiences but transcends pure autobiography by fictionalizing characters and events and injecting them with humour. And it is a journey that Wagamese continues in his remarkable *Indian Horse* (2012), a novel that ties residential school with hockey and opens by describing what happens to a family, much like Wagamese's own, when they are tragically disempowered and separated.

From the late 1980s to the 1990s and into the next decade, the list of Indigenous writers continued to grow at an unprecedented rate, and for the first time it started to become difficult to follow who was publishing what. A younger generation came into their own during this period. Dogrib writer Richard Van Camp released *The Lesser Blessed* in 1996, a coming-of-age story about Indigenous youth in the Northwest Territories, and *Angle Wing Splash Pattern* in 2002, which includes everything from popular culture to sexual awakening. In 1996, Haisla writer Eden Robinson published her first collection of urban fiction, the award-winning *Traplines*, which was described as 'disarming in its simplicity and brutal in its honesty'.[18] This description could also apply to Teetl'it Gwich'in novelist Robert Arthur Alexie's *Porcupines and China Dolls* (2002), a first novel that documents the fallout of the residential school through the lives of two survivors. Robinson's novel *Monkey Beach* (2000) might have seemed to reflect a major shift as it combines the social world of her home community of Kitamaat, British

Columbia, with the spirit world to create something entirely new (a trend she continues in her latest 'Trickster' novels[19]). But it could also be seen as part of a new focus in writing that began in Canada with Tomson Highway's play *The Rez Sisters* (1986) and was further developed in his novel *Kiss of The Fur Queen* (1998), which draws on his life, and that of his brother to explore the impact of residential school on the lives of two fictional brothers. Highway's novel blends a realism based largely on autobiography with a mythic Cree worldview to create what may be considered 'mythic-realism'.

The literary culture that shaped Highway's work had been active since 1986 when Highway, Delaware poet and playwright Daniel David Moses, and Ojibwe poet and storyteller Lenore Keeshig (Tobias) formed a loosely knit group called The Committee to Re-Establish the Trickster, uniting around the mythic Trickster figure they 'knew or re-discovered' as being common to each of their cultural traditions.[20] And in 1988, they published a quasi-political-cultural manifesto that indicated their goal to 'consolidate and gain recognition for Indigenous contributions to Canadian writing—to reclaim the Indigenous voice in literature. To facilitate the creation and production of literature by Native people.'[21] Although the publication was short-lived, the ensuing discussions around it gave Indigenous artists insight into the potential of looking backward into their own cultural traditions. It was putting theory into practice, however, that most effectively contributed to the development of Indigenous voice and a mythic or spiritual dimension to theatre and literature.

Experimenting with orality and the Trickster figure, in the 1980s Tomson Highway produced his two major plays in Toronto through Native Earth Performing Arts, *The Rez Sisters* (1986) and *Dry Lips Oughta Move To Kapuskasing* (1989). After a slow start—because no one had seen anything like it before—*The Rez Sisters* played to sold-out audiences and garnered national acclaim, as would the more controversial *Dry Lips*. The success of these plays did much to help Indigenous literature in Canada gain the critical attention of the mainstream. In a similar vein, Moses's ghost-haunted, multi-dimensional plays *Coyote City* (1988) and *Almighty Voice and His Wife* (1991) were part of this rising popularity.

Since theatre arose out of ritual and story and employed voice, movement, sound, and lighting for dramatic effect, it was readily adopted as a form of literary expression by Indigenous people, who saw it in relationship to the performances associated with the oral tradition. As Indigenous writing gained momentum, a result of the Government of Canada's multiculturalism policy of the 1970s, Indigenous theatre too began to make tentative steps during this period. The establishment of the Association for Native Development in the Performing and Visual Arts in 1972, which set up the Native Theatre School in Toronto, gave it the impetus it needed. The growing interest in theatre culminated in the establishment of two important theatre companies that changed the face of theatre in Canada: the Native Earth Performing Arts, founded in Toronto in 1982, and the Debajehmujig Theatre Group founded on Manitoulin Island in 1984. It was while working as Artistic Director for Debajehmujig during the 1984–85 season that Tomson Highway wrote and workshopped *The Rez Sisters*. The first professional production of it was through the Native Earth Performing Arts in

1986. From that point, theatre artists such as Daniel David Moses, Margo Kane, Drew Hayden Taylor, and Monique Mojica all began to develop work through either one of these theatres. Throughout the 1990s, the rapid development of Indigenous theatre was extraordinary, and it changed the landscape of Canadian drama. Contemporary Indigenous theatre has continued to flourish with the Native Earth Performing Arts' annual Weesageechak Festival developing new work, and playwrights such as Marie Clements winning awards for her distinctive experimental theatre, along with those of a newer generation like Tara Beagan making their mark. However, the degree of energy and excitement that audiences witnessed during the 'first wave' has diminished, and, although the reasons for this vary, in large part it has to do with affordable access to music and video production technology (both Clements and Beagan have written for film), which has drawn a new generation in a new direction.

Nothing happens in isolation. Although residential schools had tried in effect to sever Indigenous people from their traditions, writers from one end of the country to the other saw that these very traditions held the key to their future. They realized that you could not know where you were, and would go, without knowing where you came from. And so they began to combine historical events, like the residential school experience, and contemporary concerns with elements of traditional orature. In 1980 Thomas King arrived in Canada to teach at the University of Lethbridge, and, encountering what he calls his single greatest influence, the Okanagan stories of Harry Robinson, he began to publish fiction. In 1993, he released both his short story collection *One Good Story, That One* and his novel *Green Grass Running Water*, nominated for the Governor General's Award for Fiction that same year. Among its many attributes, King's novel shows the potential for contemporary writers to reinvent the oral tradition to tackle any number of current issues, including materialism, the environment, and political corruption. A younger generation of Indigenous writers has continued to explore and develop this genre. Today when we consider the world of the Indigenous fiction, we see that it is grounded in both the immediate present and the ancient past, in both Western and Indigenous traditions. In fact, who could have predicted the plethora of new writing that has come hand-in-hand with the new millennium? Not only have established writers like Drew Hayden Taylor, Eden Robinson, and Richard Van Camp continued to produce a steady stream of work, but so many new voices have moved into the literary landscape that for the first time it is getting difficult to keep track of them all. Just in the last few years, for example, we've had Katherena Vermette's multiple-award-winning first novel *The Break* (2016), Cherie Dimaline's Governor General's Literary Award-winning *The Marrow Thieves* (2017), Joshua Whitehead's multi-nominated *Jonny Appleseed* (2018), and Tanya Tagaq's tour de force *Split Tooth* (2018)—I could easily go on. Whether writing about family dynamics, wild ricing, gang violence, police brutality, a dystopian future, a sur/real landscape, or gender and sexuality, there is currently a profusion of exciting new writing moving in all kinds of new directions.

As fiction and drama took root in the 1980s and into the 90s, so too did poetry come into its own through access to publication and the establishment of post-secondary Indigenous literature courses across the country. It was a natural form for a people steeped in an oral tradition of music and song. It was also one of the oldest forms of literary expression adopted by Indigenous people, as shown in the work of the renowned nineteenth-century poet E. Pauline Johnson 'Tekahionwake', whom Mohawk writer Beth Brant has called 'the revolutionary . . . the spiritual grandmother . . . to those of us who are woman writers of the First Nations'.[22] (To this I would add, the spiritual grandmother to *all* Indigenous writers.) Until recent 'rediscovery' by feminists, Johnson's work was often neglected, or it was her sensual nature poetry that tended to get published at the expense of her more political poetry such as 'The Cattle Thief', which was often considered too polemical or too nationalistic to warrant publication. Unfortunately, much contemporary Indigenous poetry is met with a similar response. As the contents of this anthology demonstrate, detachment from real concerns is ideologically at odds with an Indigenous world view. Certainly, there may be exceptions, but for Indigenous poets to turn their backs on the natural world and their community would be akin to turning their backs on their cultures. To cut themselves off from their natural roots is to cut themselves off from their metaphorical ones, and vice versa. Although Indigenous poets are certainly engaged with language and poetics, more so now than ever before, it is not language for language's sake. They do not treat poetry as if it were merely a language game, a crossword puzzle to be solved or decoded, though it may at times appear that way. As tradition instructs, language is power holding the ability to change reality.

Indigenous poetry has also explicitly addressed the theme of counteracting the erasure of identity and culture. Certainly there are individual stylistic and formal differences among the poets, and yet there are nevertheless common elements found in the writing, such as a concern for language, tradition, oppression, violence, racism, materialism, and the environment. A number of the poets, for example, grapple with the idea of writing in the language of the colonizer. How could they not? They understand that this is the same language that was rammed down the throats of their forefathers and mothers and was indirectly responsible for the loss of their own Indigenous language. For while some of the Indigenous writers speak their Indigenous language, the majority do not, a result of themselves, or their parents, having attended residential school or 'burying their language' in order to survive within the dominant Anglo or Franco culture. Maria Campbell writes that for her the English language had dried up, sounding spiritless. In *Stories of the Road Allowance People* (1995), which utilizes the form of narrative poetry, she moves out of the standard English of *Halfbreed* and tells her stories in Cree-influenced and French-inflected English, 'the dialect and rhythm of my village and my father's generation'.[23] In her first collection, *Bear Bones and Feathers* (1994), Cree poet Louise Halfe employs a similar strategy in reclaiming voices that have often been dismissed as illiterate, illegitimate, and not fit for literature, and makes them powerful and healing. Likewise, Métis poet Gregory Scofield employs 'country English' and Cree in his work, most notably in his later work, *Sakihtowin-Maskihkiy Ekwa Peyak Nikamowin / Love Medicine and One Song* (1997), *I Knew Two Métis Women* (1999), and *Singing Home The Bones* (2005), while Métis poet Marilyn Dumont explores the politics of language in 'The Devil's Language', published in her award-winning first collection *A Really Good Brown Girl* (1996).

To do their job, contemporary poets have found strategies of resistance, which allow them to speak meaningfully without alienating their readers or listeners. Language serves to seduce the reader while allowing the poets to examine the often-fraught relationship between colonizer and colonized. In addressing Canadian history and a past that is in an emotional and spiritual dialogue with the present, Louise Halfe's book-length epic poem *Blue Marrow* (1998) gives voice to the 'daughters of the fur trade' who have essentially been written out of history. In her poem 'The Heat of My Grandmothers' we hear the vivid recollections of a maternal ancestor who says, 'My third husband took my calves and / gave them to the black robes . . . . Ten babies . . . . A beaded rainbow, / each child suckled by my wind-bitten nipples / their fathers loved.'[24] In my own book *Grey Owl: the Mystery of Archie Belaney* (1996), I rewrite history from an Indigenous perspective to interrogate the life of a famous Red Indian fake in the context of those who made him. As with other poets, I employ a variety of forms and devices within my text including humour and satire, which have become distinguishing features of much of Indigenous writing. Saulteaux poet Annharte's *Coyote Columbus Café* (1994) and Cree poet Marvin Francis's *city treaty: a long poem* (2002) are prime examples of satirical writing. 'I have many roles / treaty busting is like / a full time job, man,' writes Francis,[25] while Annharte concludes that 'Discovery is a hard act to follow.'[26] Both employ subversive, irreverent, scatological humour, a characteristic of 'trickster stories', deliberately borrowing 'street wise talk' to challenge and undermine the power structures that be, whether national or global.

Exemplifying a new, younger generation of Indigenous poetic voices, Liz Howard, Jordan Abel, and Billy-Ray Belcourt—three Griffin Poetry Prize winners who have taken the poetry scene by storm—reveal indisputably that Indigenous poetry is now aligned more closely than ever with Western theory. For her poetic practice, Liz Howard excavates the language of science in *Infinite Citizen of the Shaking Tent* (2015), while Jordan Abel in his collection *Injun* (2016) builds on the theories of experimental poetics to interrogate representation, and Billy-Ray Belcourt in *This Wound is a World* (2017) sets his work in a poetics of queerness, as they all grapple with issues of identity and belonging . . . and so much more. As creators and experimenters, Indigenous writers continue to give voice to a heritage of loss, pain, anger, and resistance, and, yet, at the same time, they celebrate a rich heritage of community and tradition (which they ironically and tragically may not even know). Whether writing or speaking conventional English, learned English, country English, Street talk, Rez talk, or an Indigenous language itself, Indigenous poets, writers, and storytellers strive to create balance between the present and the past, drawing on what is both contemporary and ancient, in their struggle to reaffirm their identities and cultures in Canada.

Readers familiar with Indigenous literature will be aware of the burgeoning field of literary criticism by Indigenous scholars in Canada. This is a relatively new field of writing, which has mirrored the growth of the literature itself and the increasing numbers of Indigenous scholars. The first full text of criticism solely by Indigenous people, *Looking at the Words of Our People,* was published in 1992 and edited by Jeannette Armstrong (Okanagan). In her preface, she remarks that in reading Indigenous literature there 'must first be an acknowledgement and recognition that the voices are culture-specific voices and that there are experts within those cultures who are essential' to an understanding of it. She goes on to say that Indigenous literature is indeed 'a facet of cultural practice' and that it is integral to the process of deconstructing colonialism and reconstructing Indigenous cultures. What Armstrong in fact echoes is the call for a culturally centred and ethical approach to Indigenous literature that Acoma Pueblo poet Simon Ortiz advocated in the 1980s in his essay 'Towards a National Indian Literature: Cultural Authenticity in Nationalism'.[27] I myself have written that while Indigenous literature draws strongly on Indigenous oral and spiritual traditions, it nevertheless looks at the impact of colonialism unflinchingly and 'is no less a call for liberation, survival and beyond to affirmation'.[28] Other Indigenous writers on both sides of the border have voiced similar positions. The so-called Native American literary nationalists, for example, challenge non-Native scholars who choose to write about Native American literature to keep in mind that Native Americans have been and continue to be a colonized people who struggle daily just to survive, and as such they advocate that tribal/pan-tribal knowledge and experience are not only valid, but even necessary in addressing a nation's literature. The concept of nationhood itself is linked to community values, histories, and traditions within a tribal specific understanding of humankind's bond of kinship to one another and the natural world. And, further, when non-Indigenous scholars get lost in the cant of authenticity or Western theory, such as hybridity theory, this ultimately serves to deracinate and further colonize Indigenous peoples. Although the 'debates' around such issues as whether or not something called 'Indigenous literature' can even exist in an increasingly multicultural world (or, for that matter, who has the right to claim Indigenous identity), whether it can exist outside of nation- or tribal-specific contexts, and how one should approach it critically, have only recently made their way across the American border and into scholarly discourse, Indigenous literary nationalism in Canada is not new. One only has to turn to any number of the writers in this anthology. For example, one may consider the 1970s writing of Howard Adams (Métis), Harold Cardinal (Cree), and Emma LaRocque (Cree/Métis)—along with recent writers who have all been added to this edition—to come to some understanding of the roots and continuing development of this movement here in Canada. And I might add that it continues to influence Indigenous creative expression and move it in directions that warrant address, indicative of the new work included in this edition, addressing issues around violence against Indigenous women and girls, and gender.

And finally, a word about the process of anthologizing itself, which necessarily raises the issue of canonization, something the editors of the first edition briefly address in their dialogue. Daniel David Moses referred to the process of deciding what should be included as a political decision rather than an aesthetic one, based on the 'impact' of the writing, while acknowledging the difficulty of putting together an anthology 'with a literature that is emerging as we speak'.[29] Terry Goldie went so far as to say that he 'would feel personally a bit of a failure if people thought that it . . . establishes what is the best in Native writing, or even establishes what is the best in Native writing in 1992.'[30] I still agree completely with both my former co-editors and point to the limitations of space and other imposed parameters placed on the text. Canadian poet and novelist Michael Ondaatje remarks in his introduction to *From Ink Lake*, which incidentally also came out in the early 1990s and includes Indigenous authors, 'An anthologist goes mad trying to be fair and dutiful and must at some point relinquish that responsibility.'[31] In compiling his own idiosyncratic selection, he concludes with what might be considered an escape hatch. He says, 'I emphasized from the start, this anthology is more a reader, a sampling, than my attempt at an official canon.'[32] In regard to this fifth edition of the anthology, I (again) often found myself looking for a quick getaway when I thought that I might be creating an official canon, and so I too state unequivocally that this anthology is but a sampling of the incredible diversity of writing that is out there for readers to discover for themselves. This brings me to the 'Timeline' I have put together (reviewed by my co-editor) that marks some of the major moments in the literature while giving readers a 'bird's eye view' of its development since contact. What we see are a few lone voices extending back nearly two centuries politely asking to be heard, struggling to hold on to the last vestiges of land and culture, voices slowly gathering momentum and transforming into resounding protest, transforming again and again, to become a chorus of disparate voices, who together have created the field of study we now call 'Indigenous Literature'. This of course is nothing less than remarkable when one considers that it has occurred despite everything that has been done by Church and State during the last two centuries to silence these voices. That the Timeline illustrates succinctly where the literature has come from and where it is, perhaps by intimation, may also give us an inkling of where it is going. Chi-Miigwech.

Notes

1. Armand Garnet Ruffo, 'Where the Voice Was Coming From', in *Across Cultures Across Borders: Canadian Aboriginal and Native American Literatures,* ed. Paul DePasquale, Renate Eigenbrod, and Emma LaRocque, 182.
2. Basil Johnston, 'Is That All There Is? Tribal Literature', in *An Anthology of Canadian Native Literature in English,* ed. Daniel David Moses and Terry Goldie, 107.
3. Canada, Department of Indian Affairs and Northern Development, 'Statement of the Government of Canada on Indian Policy, 1969', in *Expressions in Canadian Native Studies,* ed. Ron F. Laliberte et al., 529–46.
4. Jennifer David, 'Interview with Maria Campbell', in *Storykeepers* (pilot for documentary film series, 2005).
5. Kenneth Lincoln, *Native American Renaissance.* Berkley: University of California Press, 1983.
6. Thomas King, 'Introduction', in *All My Relations*, xiv.
7. Basil Johnston, *The Manitous: The Spiritual World of The Ojibway,* xii.

8. Joseph Brant, 'Letter', in *An Anthology of Canadian Native Literature in English*, ed. Daniel David Moses and Terry Goldie, 14.
9. Catherine Soneegoh Sutton, ibid., 25.
10. George Copway, *The Life of Kah-Ge-Ga-Gah-Bowh*, ibid., 23.
11. Jeannette C. Armstrong, 'The Disempowerment of First North American Native Peoples and Empowerment Through Their Writing', ibid., 244.
12. Rita Joe, 'I Lost My Talk', in *An Anthology of Canadian Native Literature in English*, 113.
13. Basil Johnston, 'One Generation from Extinction' and 'Is That All There Is? Tribal Literature', in *An Anthology of Canadian Native Literature in English*, 92–105.
14. Louise Halfe, 'Residential School Alumni', in *Burning In This Midnight Dream*, Regina: Coteau Books, 2016.
15. Rosanna Deerchild, 'bread crumbs', in *calling down the sky*, Regina: Coteau Books, 2015.
16. Lenore Keeshig-Tobias, 'After Oka—How Has Canada Changed?' ibid., 257.
17. Paul Seesequasis, 'The Republic of Tricksterism', ibid., 468.
18. Eden Robinson, 'Review', *Independent on Sunday* in *Traplines*, New York: Vintage Canada, 1996.
19. Eden Robinson, *Son of A Trickster*, 2017; *Trickster Drift*, 2018.
20. Daniel David Moses, 'The Trickster's Laugh: My Meeting with Tomson and Lenore', in *American Indian Quarterly* 28, no. 1/2, (2004): 108, 111.
21. Lenore Keeshig Tobias, 'Introduction', in *The Magazine to Re-Establish the Trickster* 1, no. 1 (1988).
22. Beth Brant, 'The Good Red Road: Journey's of Homecoming in Native Women's Writing', in *Writing As Witness: Essay and Talk*, 7.
23. Maria Campbell, 'Introduction', in *Stories of The Road Allowance People*, 2.
24. Louise Halfe, 'The Heat of My Grandmothers', in *An Anthology of Canadian Native Literature in English*, 403–4.
25. Marvin Francis, 'BNA ACTOR', in *An Anthology of Canadian Native Literature in English*, 433–5.
26. Annharte, 'Coyote Columbus Café', in *An Anthology of Canadian Native Literature in English*, 182–6.
27. Simon J. Ortiz, 'Towards a National Indian Literature: Cultural Authenticity in Nationalism', in *American Indian Literary Nationalism*, eds. Jace Weaver, Craig S. Womack and Robert Warrior, 253–60.
28. Armand Garnet Ruffo, 'Why Native Literature?' *American Indian Quarterly* 21, no. 4 (Fall 1997): 663–73.
29. Daniel David Moses, 'Preface to the First Edition: Two Voices', in *An Anthology of Canadian Native Literature in English*, xiv.
30. Terry Goldie, 'Preface to the First Edition: Two Voices', in *An Anthology of Canadian Native Literature in English*, xiv.
31. Michael Ondaatje, 'Introduction', in *From Ink Lake*, ed. Michael Ondaatje, xiii.
32. Michael Ondaatje, ibid., xvii.

Bibliography

Armstrong, Jeannette. *Looking at The Words of Our People: First Nations Analysis of Literature*. Penticton: Theytus Books, 1993.

Campbell, Maria. *Stories of The Road Allowance People*. Penticton: Theytus Books, 1995.

DePasquale, Paul, Renate Eigenbrod, and Emma LaRocque. *Across Cultures Across Borders: Canadian Aboriginal and Native American Literatures*. Peterborough: Broadview Press, 2010.

Johnston, Basil. *The Manitous: The Spiritual World of The Ojibway*. Toronto: KeyPorter Books, 1995.

King, Thomas, ed. *All My Relations*. Toronto: McClelland and Stewart, 1990.

Laliberte, Ron. F, et al., eds. *Expressions in Canadian Native Studies*. Saskatoon: University of Saskatchewan, 2000.

Lincoln, Kenneth. *Native American Renaissance*. Berkley: University of California Press, 1983.

Moses, Daniel David, 'The Trickster's Laugh: My Meeting with Tomson and Lenore.' *American Indian Quarterly* 28.1/2, 2004.

Moses, Daniel David and Terry Goldie, eds. *An Anthology of Canadian Native Literature in English*. Toronto: Oxford University Press, 1992.

Ondaatje, Michael, ed. *From Ink Lake*. Toronto: Lester & Orpen Dennys, 1990.

Robinson, Eden. *Traplines: Stories*. New York: Vintage Canada, 1996.

Tobias, Lenore Keeshig, 'Introduction.' *The Magazine to Re-Establish the Trickster* 1.1, 1988.

Weaver, Jace, Craig S. Womack, and Robert Warrior. *American Indian Literary Nationalism*. Albuquerque: University of New Mexico Press, 2005.

Traditional Orature

Southern First Nations

While the majority of pieces collected here are writings by Indigenous authors, the cultural roots of this literature are in traditional orature. The term 'orature' is chosen as a parallel to the term 'literature'. Orature indicates that body of knowledge usually referred to as 'oral literature'. The latter term is problematic, including as it does the words 'literature', with its implications of reading and books, and 'oral', with implications of the spoken and heard. 'Oral literature' seems a debased version of a true written literature. The term 'orature' allows this body of knowledge its own validity.

It is tempting to emphasize authenticity in a consideration of traditional material, but this is generally counterproductive. If 'authentic' implies without change through white contact, there is no such account of traditional cultures from southern Canada. The first considered white accounts of Indigenous cultures long postdate the first contact.

We have used early versions of poems and songs as they were recorded, usually by amateur folklorists, to suggest the cultural and aesthetic roots of this collection. All the examples here come from John Robert Colombo's *Songs of the Indians*, which provides interesting notes and comments about the material, both general and specific. The verse forms and word usage more likely reflect English literary values than Indigenous ones, but their provenance gives them clear historical positions. They are also of interest as demonstrations of various cultural tensions. As an example, here are some comments made by the famous American folklorist and collector Charles G. Leland, in *The Algonquin Legends of New England*, on a piece provided by Mrs W. Wallace Brown of Calais, Maine:

The old woman ended this story by saying abruptly, 'Don't know any more. Guess they all eat up by *mooin*' (the bear). She said it was only a fragment. 'If you could have heard her repeat this,' adds Mrs Brown, 'in pieces, stopping to explain what the characters said, and describing how they looked, and anon singing it again, you would have got the *inner sense* of a wonderfully weird tale. The woman's feet-covering and the man's dress *like* a rainbow, yet not one, which made their bodies invisible, seemed to exercise her imagination strangely; and these were to her the most important part of the story.' The fragment is part of a very old myth; I regret to say a very obscure one. The poem, 'declared to be very ancient', is given here as 'Fragment of a Passamaquoddy song'.

The section given here from 'Traditional History of the Confederacy of Six Nations' is a different example of the problem of authenticity. As Colombo notes, 'This official version of the oral tradition was prepared by a Committee of the Chiefs at the Six Nations Reserve, Grand River, at the turn of the century.' Like the material presented by traditional storytellers today, it has the authenticity of all oral material that is reaffirmed through its transmission within a cultural tradition.

While authenticity might be impossible, contemporary scholarship continues to work to find ways to improve the representation of orature. In the present volume, we draw your attention to the selections from Ghandl, Louis Bird, and Harry Robinson. For a more general view, see the anthology *Voices from*

Four Directions: Contemporary Translations of the Native Literatures of North America (2004), edited by Brian Swann. Robert Bringhurst's collection of translations, *A Story Sharp as a Knife: The Classic Haida Mythtellers and Their World* (1999), is an excellent introduction to orature in general, and the bibliography offers many possibilities for research.

Song for Medicine Hunting

Now I hear it, my friends, of the Metai, who are sitting about me.
Who makes this river flow? The Spirit, he makes this river flow.
Look at me well, my friends; examine me, and let me understand that we are
    all compassion.
Who maketh to walk about the social people? A birth maketh to walk about
    the social people.
I fly about, and if anywhere I see an animal, I can shoot him.   5
I shoot your heart; I hit your heart, oh animal, your heart, I hit your heart.
I make myself look like fire.
I am able to call water from above, from beneath, and from around.
I cause to look like the dead, a man I did.
I cause to look like the dead, a woman I did.   10
I cause to look like the dead, a child I did.
I am such, I am such, my friends; any animal, any animal, my friends,
    I hit him right, my friends.

Traditional History of the Confederacy

CONSTITUTION

Then Dekanahwideh said, Now I and you Lords of the Confederate Nations shall plant a Great Tall and Mighty Tree of the Great Long Leaves.

    Now this Tree which we have planted shall shoot forth four great long white roots. These Great Long White Roots shall shoot forth one to the North and one to the South and one to the East and one to the West, and we shall place on the top of it an Eagle which has a great power of long vision, and we shall transact all our business under the shade of the Great Tree. The meaning of planting this Great Tree is the Great Peace, and Good Tidings of Peace and Power, and the Nations of the earth shall see it and shall accept and follow the Root and shall arrive here at this Tree and when they arrive here you shall receive them and shall seat them in the midst of your Confederacy, and the meaning of placing an Eagle on the top of the Great Tall Tree is to watch the Roots which extend to the North and to the South and to the East and to the West, and the Eagle will discover if any evil is approaching your Confederacy, and will scream and give the alarm and all the Nations of the Confederacy at once shall hear the alarm and come to the front.

    Then Dekanahwideh said again, We shall now combine our Power into one Great Power which is this Confederacy, and we shall now therefore symbolize the union of these powers by each Nation contributing one arrow each which we shall tie up together in a bundle, which when it is made and completely tied together no-one can bend or break it.

Then Dekanahwideh further said, We have now completed this union in securing one arrow from each Nation, it is not good that one should be lacking or taken from the bundle, for it would weaken our power and it would be still worse if two arrows were taken from the bundle. And if three arrows were taken, then any one could break the remaining arrows in the bundle.

Then Dekanahwideh continued his address and said, We shall now therefore tie this bundle of arrows together with deer's sinew which is strong, durable and lasting and then this Institution will be strong and unchangeable. This bundle of arrows signifies that all Lords and all the Warriors and all the Women of the Confederacy have become united as one person.

Then Dekanahwideh said, We have now completed our power so that we, the Five Nations Confederacy, shall in the future only have one body, one head and one heart.

Then he further said, If any evil should befall us in the future we shall stand or fall unitedly as one man.

CONDOLENCE CEREMONY

Now hear us our Uncles, we have come to condole with you in your great bereavement.

We have now met in dark sorrow to lament together over the death of our brother Lord. For such has been your loss. We will sit together in our grief and mingle our tears together, and we four brothers will wipe off the tears from your eyes, so that for a day period you might have peace of mind. This we say and do, we four brothers.

Now hear us again, for when a person is in great grief caused by death, his ears are closed up and he cannot hear, and such is your condition now.

We will therefore remove the obstruction from your ears, so that for a day period you may have perfect hearing again. This we say and do, we four brothers.

Continue to bear the expression of us four brothers, for when a person is in great sorrow his throat is stopped with grief and such is your case now. We will therefore remove the obstruction so that for a day period you may enjoy perfect breathing and speech. This we say and do, we four brothers.

The foregoing part of the Condolence Ceremony is to be performed outside of the place of meeting.

HAIL

I come to greet and thank my uncles,
I come again to greet and thank the League;
I come again to greet and thank the Kindred;
I come again to greet and thank the Warriors;

I come again to greet and thank the Women;
My forefathers—what they established—
My forefathers—hearken to them.

AT THE WOOD'S EDGE

Oh, my grandsires! Even now that has become old which you established—the Great League. You have it as a pillow under your heads in the ground where you are lying—this Great League which you established; although you said that far away in the future the Great League would endure.

*   *   *

Now listen, ye who established the Great League of Peace. Now it has become old. Now there is nothing but wilderness. Ye are in your graves who established it. Yet have taken it with you and have placed it under you, and there is nothing left but a desert. There ye have taken your intellects with joy. What ye established ye have taken with you. Ye have placed under your heads what ye established—the Great League.

Song for the Burning of the White Dog

Great Master, behold here are all of our people who hold the old faith, and who intend to abide by it.

By means of this dog being burned we hope to please Thee, and that just as we have decked it with ribbons and wampum, Thou wilt grant favours to us Thy own people.

I now place the dog on the fire that its spirit may find its way to Thee who made it, and made everything, and thus we hope to get blessings from Thee in return.

He throws the dog on the fire and proceeds:

Although, Great Master, there are not so many of us who worship Thee in this way as there were in old times, those who are here are as faithful as ever—now, therefore, listen to us—Thou who art far away above us, and who made every living thing.

We ask that the sun will continue to shine on us and make all things grow.

We ask that the moon may always give us light by night.

We ask that the clouds may never cease to give us rain or snow.

We ask that the winds from the east and west and north and south may always blow.

We ask that the trees and everything that springs from the ground may grow. We ask that these blessings may help us through life, and that we may remain true to our belief in Thee, and we will make Thee another offering like this next year.

Save us from all harm until that time, and make us obedient to our chiefs and others who have power.

Guide them so that they may act wisely for the people and save them from all harm.

Be good, Great Master, to the warriors and to the young men, making them strong and healthy so that they may always be able to do everything they ought to do.

Great Master, we ask also that Thou wouldst be kind to the women until our next feast. Make them strong and healthy so that they may always be able to do everything they ought to do.

Take away all our sickness and all our troubles. Make us happy and healthy and strong to enjoy life.

Great Master, make us all peaceable and kindly that we may live happily and contentedly as we should do.

Cause the plants that cure us when we are ill to grow up strong for our use so that they do what Thou madest them to do.

And, Great Master, may the coming season bring us plenty of sunshine and breezes, and may everything grow well for our use during the summer time.

May all the trees that bear fruit, and may everything that comes out of the ground as our food grow in the best way for us to enjoy.

Great Master, we ask, too, that Thou wouldst send us all sorts of animals, large and small, for food and clothing, and cause the birds to live and increase in number.

May the scent of the tobacco I have thrown on the fire rise till it reaches Thee to let Thee know that we are still good—that we do not forget Thee, and that Thou mayest give us all we have asked.

Traditional Songs

Inuit

Much of the note on traditional orature from the Southern First Nations can be applied here, with the exception that the records here date from much later. These songs are again taken from a collection by John Robert Colombo, *Poems of the Inuit* (1981). Colombo's primary source was Knud Rasmussen, but all of his sources were from the twentieth century. One might assume that the combination of the greater isolation of the Inuit with developments in scientific ethnography should make for greater accuracy. But by the same token, the Inuit's isolation from the white culture that had had centuries to influence other First Nations by the time their traditional material was collected, made the Inuit that much more difficult for white explorers to begin to understand. Thus, it once again would be best to assume that accuracy is not to be found, and to see these as samples of a recording process that comments on both cultures involved.

My Breath/Orpingalik

I will sing a song,
A song that is strong.
    Unaya—unaya.
Sick I have lain since autumn,

Helpless I lay, as were I 5
My own child.

Sad, I would that my woman
Were away to another house
To a husband
Who can be her refuge, 10
Safe and secure as winter ice.
    Unaya—unaya.

Sad, I would that my woman
Were gone to a better protector
Now that I lack strength 15
To rise from my couch.
    Unaya—unaya.

Dost thou know thyself?
So little thou knowest of thyself.
Feeble I lie here on my bench 20
And only my memories are strong!
    Unaya—unaya.

Beasts of the hunt! Big game!
Oft the fleeting quarry I chased!
Let me live it again and remember, 25
Forgetting my weakness.
    Unaya—unaya.

Let me recall the great white
Polar bear,
High up its black body, 30
Snout in the snow, it came!
He really believed
He alone was a male
And ran toward me.
    Unaya—unaya. 35

It threw me down
Again and again,
Then breathless departed
And lay down to rest,
Hid by a mound on a floe. 40
Heedless it was, and unknowing
That I was to be its fate.

Deluding itself
That he alone was a male,
And unthinking   45
That I too was a man!
    Unaya—unaya.

I shall ne'er forget that great blubber-beast,
A fjord seal,
I killed from the sea ice   50
Early, long before dawn,
While my companions at home
Still lay like the dead,
Faint from failure and hunger,
Sleeping.   55
With meat and with swelling blubber
I returned so quickly
As if merely running over ice
To view a breathing hole there.
And yet it was   60
An old and cunning male seal.
But before he had even breathed
My harpoon head was fast
Mortally deep in his neck.

That was the manner of me then.   65
Now I lie feeble on my bench
Unable even a little blubber to get
For my wife's stone lamp.
The time, the time will not pass,
While dawn gives place to dawn   70
And spring is upon the village.
    Unaya—unaya.

But how long shall I lie here?
How long?
And how long must she go a-begging   75
For fat for her lamp,
For skins for clothing
And meat for a meal?
A helpless thing—a defenceless woman.
    Unaya—unaya.   80

Knowest thou thyself?
So little thou knowest of thyself!

While dawn gives place to dawn,
And spring is upon the village.
    Unaya—unaya. 85

Magic Words/Aua

To Lighten Heavy Loads

I speak with the mouth of Qeqertuanaq, and say:
I will walk with leg muscles strong as the sinews on the shin of a little
    caribou calf.
I will walk with leg muscles strong as the sinews on the shin of a little hare.
I will take care not to walk toward the dark.
I will walk toward the day.

To Cure Sickness Among Neighbours

I arise from my couch with the grey gull's morning song.
I arise from my couch with the grey gull's morning song.
I will take care not to look toward the dark,
I will turn my glance toward the day.

To Cure a Sick Child

Little Child! Your mother's breasts are full of milk.
Go to her and suck, go to her and drink. Go up into the mountain.
From the mountain's top shalt thou find health; from the mountain's top
    shalt thou win life.

To Stop Bleeding

This is blood from the little sparrow's mother.
Dry it up! This is blood that flowed from a piece of wood. Dry it up!

For Calling Game to the Hunter

Beast of the sea! Come and place yourself before me in the dear early
    morning!
Beast of the plain! Come and place yourself before me in the dear early
    morning!

Magic Words/Nakasuk

To Heal Wounds

You, like a ringed plover,
You, like a wild duck,
The skin's surface here,
Full of wounds,
Full of cuts,   5
Go and patch it!

Song of the Girl Who Was Turning into Stone/Ivaluardjuk

Men in kayaks,
come hither to me
and be my husbands;
this stone here
has clung fast to me,   5
and lo, my feet
are now turning to stone.

Men in kayaks,
come hither to me
and be my husbands;   10
this stone here
has clung fast to me,
and lo, my legs
are now turning to stone.

Men in kayaks,   15
come hither to me
and be my husbands;
this stone here
has clung fast to me,
and lo, now my thighs   20
are turning to stone.

Men in kayaks,
come hither to me
and be my husbands;
this stone here   25
has clung fast to me,

and lo, from the waist down,
I am turning to stone.

Men in kayaks,
come hither to me   30
and be my husbands;
this stone here
has clung fast to me,
and lo, my entrails
are turning to stone.   35

Men in kayaks,
come hither to me
and be my husbands;
this stone here
has clung fast to me,   40
and lo, my lungs
are now turning to stone.

Dead Man's Song/Netsit

Dreamed by One Who is Alive

I am filled with joy
When the day peacefully dawns
Up over the heavens,
    ayi, yai ya.

I am filled with joy   5
When the sun slowly rises
Up over the heavens,
    ayi, yai ya.

But else I choke with fear
At greedy maggot throngs;   10
They eat their way in
At the hollow of my collarbone
And in my eyes,
    ayi, yai ya.

Here I lie, recollecting   15
How stifled with fear I was

When they buried me
In a snow hut out on the lake,
    ayi, yai ya.

A block of snow was pushed to, 20
Incomprehensible it was
How my soul should make its way
And fly to the game land up there,
    ayi, yai ya.

That door-block worried me, 25
And ever greater grew my fear
When the fresh-water ice split in the cold,
And the frost-crack thunderously grew
Up over the heavens,
    ayi, yai ya. 30

Glorious was life
In winter.
But did winter bring me joy?
No! Ever was I so anxious
For sole-skins and skins for kamiks, 35
Would there be enough for us all?
Yes, I was ever anxious,
    ayi, yai ya.

Glorious was life
In summer. 40
But did summer bring me joy?
No! Ever was I so anxious
For skins and rugs for the platform,
Yes, I was ever anxious,
    ayi, yai ya. 45

Glorious was life
When standing at one's fishing-hole
On the ice.
But did standing at the fishing-hole bring me joy?
No! Ever was I so anxious 50
For my tiny little fish-hook
If it should not get a bite,
    ayi, yai ya.

Glorious was life
When dancing in the dance-house. 55
But did dancing in the dance-house bring me joy?
No! Ever was I so anxious,
That I could not recall
The song I was to sing.
Yes, I was ever anxious, 60
   ayi, yai ya.

Glorious was life. . . .
Now I am filled with joy
For every time a dawn
Makes white the sky of night, 65
For every time the sun goes up
Over the heavens,
   ayi, yai ya.

Joseph Brant c. 1742–1807

Mohawk

Joseph Brant, Thayendanegea, was born in what is now Ohio in either 1742 or 1743. He was with Sir William Johnson as early as his expedition against Fort Niagara during the Seven Years' War (1759) and in 1761 was sent as Johnson's protegé to Moor's Indian Charity School for two years. In the following years Brant acted as an interpreter for Johnson, for his successor Guy Johnson, and for missionaries.

  A Loyalist, after the outbreak of the American Revolution he chose to lead Indigenous forces as a war chief against the Americans. Following the Revolution he worked to create a new confederacy of Indigenous peoples to block American expansion westward.

  In 1784 Brant led a group of Mohawk Loyalists to a settlement on the Grand River (named Brant's ford in 1827, now Brantford), in what is now Ontario. The land was a grant given by the British in compensation for loss of land in the United States, and for support of the British cause. Brant's activities have had longstanding repercussions. For example, his conviction that the Indigenous future must be tied to developing white methods of agriculture and his attempt to lease land to whites in order to gain working capital resulted in extended conflict with both Indigenous people and the government. He died in Burlington, Ontario.

  Brant is better known as a figure in literature than as an author. His Christianity, his Loyalism, his statesmanship, and his military reputation have made him a perfect subject for depiction as a 'noble savage'. These portraits range from the nineteenth-century closet drama *Thayendanegea*, by J.B. Mackenzie, to the television miniseries *Divided Loyalties*. Still, Brant, who in his later years worked to translate the Bible into Mohawk, devoted significant energy to his words as a statesman, as is typical of Indigenous politicians from the oratory of precontact culture to the essays and speeches of Indigenous leaders today. The following examples of his writing embrace sophisticated rhetorical principles, with a forthright commitment to the power of language.

Letter

Sir,   Grand River, Dec. 10, 1798

Our former acquaintance encourages me to take the freedom of writing you; but knowing the multiplicity of business you have on your hands, I would not trouble you with this, did not the particular situation of our affairs seem to require it, thinking it necessary for me candidly to acquaint my friends with the feelings of my mind.

    I presume that you are well acquainted with the long difficulties we had concerning the lands on this river—these difficulties we had not the least idea of when we first settled here, looking on them as granted us to be indisputably our own, otherwise we would never have accepted the lands, yet afterwards it seemed a little odd to us that the writings Gov. Haldimand gave us after our settling on the lands, was not so compleat as the strong assurances and promises he had made us at first, but this made no great impression on our minds, still confiding in the goodness of his Majesty's intentions, and in the weight we caputed our former services would have with him—Had it not been for this confidence and affection we bore the Kings we still had opportunities left after the war, in providing for ourselves in the free and independent manner natural to Indians, unhappily for us we have been made acquainted too late with the first real intentions of Ministry; that is, that they never intended us to have it in our power to alienate any part of the lands; and here we have even been prohibited from taking tenants on them, it having been represented as inconsistent for us, being but King's allies, to have King's subjects as tenants, consequently I suppose their real meaning was, we should in a manner be but tenants ourselves, as for me I see no difference in it any farther than that we are as yet rent free—they seemingly intending to forbid us any other use of the lands than that of sitting down or walking on them. It plainly appears by this that their motives can be no other than to tie us down in such a manner, as to have us entirely at their disposal for whatever services they may in future want from us, and that in case we should be worried out, and obliged to move the lands would then fall to them with our improvements of labour.

    Sir, I hope I shall not tire your patience, in making a few remarks on what I suppose may naturally be the thoughts of Government on our conduct—With respect to myself they might say he has half pay and yet talks so much on these matters, it is very true I enjoy that bounty of his Majesty, so many worthless fellows like me do, that have never risked their property or any thing else in his causes but am I for this entirely to forsake the interests of my people? that put their dependence on me besides my family which is very numerous cannot be benefitted by my half pay when I am no more; which at my time of life I have reason to look on as a period not so very distant. I think it therefore incumbent on me to secure what they must look to for a future support. With respect to the Nation they may also say, that they have received their losses, for instance our hunting grounds that were very extensive, besides several other tracts of land were never mentioned—The Miller, blacksmith, and School-master, that is allowed us by government may also be spoken of—we are indeed very thankful for it; but we look upon this as all temporary and the continuance of it to be uncertain—it may likewise be said they receive annual presents what do they want more, we gratefully thank his Majesty, for his bounty in this respect; but I am sorry to have to observe that this goes very little ways in clothing the poor and helpless—and the country is so much changed that hunting is of very little account to the young and robust.

    I beg to say a few words more on this subject, the movements of Gov. Simcoe in attempting to curtail our lands to one half of the River, and recollecting our deed from Gov. Haldimand to be unequal to his first promises caused us to make such a large sale at once that the matter might come to a point and we might know whether the land was ours or not—the next reason was, that the lands all round us being given away to different people, some of them, those that had even been engaged in war against us, we found it necessary to sell some land, that we might have an income, the hunting being entirely destroyed.—We now learn that the ministry never intended we should alienate the lands, alleging that by doing so, disaffected people might be introduced into the country that might injure government—the people we have sold the lands to are loyalist & we expect, that as other people settled in the province, they will become subjects to His Majesty, the same as if Gov. Simcoe had himself curtailed the land and given it to them, as he has done with the adjacent lands.

I am sorry for having taken up so much of your time with so tedious a letter but I assure my present disagreeable situation, affects my feelings so much, that I cannot avoid expressing it rather fully especially as I think this shall be the last time I will trouble you on the subject. Capt. Green	Sir I am Your most obed^t and Humb. Servt. Jos. Brant

[1798]

Condolence Speech

To Captain Claus on the death of his mother (Ann Johnson Claus) made by Captain Joseph Brant, 24 February 1801 at Fort George.

Brother! We are here now met in the presence of the Spirit above, with the intent to keep up the ancient custom of condolement. We therefore condole with you for your late loss of our well beloved sister, whom now you have interred.

    Brother! We hope that this may not damp your heart so much as to make you forget us, who are your brothers, not only ourselves but our wives and children.

Brother! We say now again that by our late loss it seems our fire is somewhat extinguished. But now we have found a few brands remaining and have collected them together and have raised a straight smoke to the clouds.

Brother! We therefore with this string of Wampum wipe away the tears from your eyes and would take away all sorrow from your heart. But that is impossible, still it is the customary way of making the speech. We, therefore, mention it and with the said Wampum we wipe away all stains of whatever should remain on your seat so that you may sit down in comfort.

Brother! We say again with this string of Wampum, as you seem to be all in darkness, we with the same string enlighten the skies about us so that it may appear to us all as it formerly used to do.

Brother! We say again with this string of Wampum as we now have made our speech of condolement, we hope to raise you upon your feet as you formerly used to be for since our late loss it seems you have been confined as one absent.

Brother! We hope you will not forget our calamities; hoping that this shock may not put us out of your memory entirely; and also that you may continue to keep us as you formerly used to do.

Brother! This last string which now I give you is given by the whole Six Nations so as to strengthen your mind and body that you may not be cast down by the occasion of our late loss.

[1801]

George Copway 1818-1869

Mississauga Anishinaabe

George Copway, Kahgegagahbowh ('He Who Stands Forever'), was born near what is now Trenton, Ontario. His father, a medicine man and one of the chiefs of the Rice Lake Indian Village, was converted by Indigenous Methodist missionaries in 1827, as was his mother soon after. George converted in 1830, at the age of twelve, and began work as a teacher in 1834. He was sent to Jacksonville, Illinois, in 1836 to study for two years at the Ebenezer Methodist Seminary. He became an ordained minister and travelled with his English wife as a missionary to Indigenous communities in both the United States and Canada. When two First Nation bands in Canada accused him of embezzlement, the Methodists expelled him, and in 1846 he returned to the United States, where he became a successful lecturer and author.

Copway translated part of the Bible into Ojibwe, but his major literary achievement was his autobiography, *The Life, History, and Travels of Kah-ge-ga-gah-bowh* (1847), from which the following selections are taken. It was the first book in English written by a Canadian Indigenous person. Copway also wrote *The Traditional History and Characteristic Sketches of the Ojibwa Nation* (1850) and *Running Sketches of Men and Places in England, France, Germany, Belgium and Scotland* (1851)—an account of his European travels—and edited the short-lived weekly *Copway's American Indian* (1851).

Copway had prominent supporters in the United States, including James Fenimore Cooper, Washington Irving, Henry Wadsworth Longfellow, Francis Parkman, and Henry Rowe Schoolcraft. His books were popular successes, with his autobiography published in six editions. That book's antipaganism and passionate faith in conversion seem obsessive today, but Copway's attacks on British and American Indigenous policy and his imaginative proposals on land rights were decidedly progressive.

A Word to the Reader

It would be presumptuous in one, who has but recently been brought out of a wild and savage state; and who has since received but three years' schooling, to undertake, without any assistance, to publish to the world a work of any kind. It is but a few years since I began to speak the English language. An unexpected opportunity occurred of submitting my manuscript to a friend, who has kindly corrected all *serious* grammatical errors, leaving the unimportant ones wholly untouched, that my own style may be exhibited as truly as possible. The public and myself are indebted to him for his kind aid, and he has my most sincere thanks. The language, (except in a few short sentences,) the plan, and the arrangement are all my own; and I am wholly responsible for all the statements, and the remaining defects. My work is now accomplished; and I am too well aware of the many faults which are still to be found therein. Little could I imagine, that I should have to contend with so many obstacles. All along, have I felt my great deficiency; and my inadequacy for such an undertaking. I would fain hope, however, that the kind Reader will throw the mantle of charity over errors of every kind. I am a stranger in a strange land! And often, when the sun is sinking in the western sky, I think of my former home; my heart yearns for the loved of other days, and tears flow like the summer rain. How the heart of the wanderer and pilgrim, after long years of absence, beats, and his eyes fill, as he catches a glance at the hills of his nativity, and reflects upon the time when he pressed the lips of a mother, or sister, now cold in death. Should I live, this painful pleasure will yet be mine. *'Blessed be the Lord, who hath helped me hitherto.'*

KAH-GE-GA-GAH-BOWH,
ALIAS
GEORGE COPWAY
July 1847.

[1847]

The Life of Kah-Ge-Ga-Gah-Bowh

The Christian will no doubt feel for my poor people, when he hears the story of one brought from that unfortunate race called the Indians. The lover of humanity will be glad to see that that once powerful race can be made to enjoy the blessings of life.

What was once impossible—or rather thought to be—is made possible through my experience. I have made many close observations of men, and things around me;

but, I regret to say, that I do not think I have made as good use of my opportunities as I might have done. It will be seen that I know but little—yet O how precious *that little!*—I would rather lose my right hand than be deprived of it.

I loved the woods, and the chase. I had the nature for it, and gloried in nothing else. The mind for letters was in me, *but was asleep*, till the dawn of Christianity arose, and awoke the slumbers of the soul into energy and action.

You will see that I served the imaginary gods of my poor blind father. I was out early and late in quest of the favours of the *Mon-e-doos* (spirits,) who, it was said, were numerous—who filled the air! At early dawn I watched the rising of the *palace* of the Great Spirit—*the sun*—who, it was said, made the world!

Early as I can recollect, I was taught that it was the gift of the many spirits to be a good hunter and warrior; and much of my time I devoted in search of their favours. On the mountain top, or along the valley, or the water brook, I searched for some kind of intimation from the spirits who made their residence in the noise of the waterfalls.

I dreaded to hear the voice of the angry spirit in the gathering clouds. I looked with anxiety to catch a glimpse of the wings of the Great Spirit, who shrouded himself in rolling white and dark clouds—who, with his wings, fanned the earth, and laid low the tall pines and hemlock in his course—who rode in whirlwinds and tornadoes, and plucked the trees from their woven roots—who chased other gods from his course—who drove the Bad Spirit from the surface of the earth, down to the dark caverns of the deep. Yet he was a kind spirit. My father taught me to call that spirit Ke-sha-mon-e-doo—*Benevolent spirit*—for his ancestors taught him no other name to give to that spirit who made the earth, with all its variety and smiling beauty. His benevolence I saw in the running of the streams, for the animals to quench their thirst and the fishes to live; the fruit of the earth teemed wherever I looked. Every thing I saw smilingly said Ke-sha-mon-e-doo nin-ge-oo-she-ig—*the Benevolent spirit made me.*

Where is he? My father pointed to the sun. What is his will concerning me, and the rest of the Indian race? This was a question that I found no one could answer, until a beam from heaven shone on my pathway, which was very dark, when first I saw that there was a true heaven—not in the far-setting sun, where the Indian anticipated a rest, a home for his spirit—but in the bosom of the Highest.

I view my life like the mariner on the wide ocean, without a compass, in the dark night, as he watches the heavens for the north star, which his eye having discovered, he makes his way amidst surging seas, and tossed by angry billows into the very jaws of death, till he arrives safely anchored at port. I have been tossed with hope and fear in this life; no star-light shone on my way, until the men of God pointed me to a Star in the East, as it rose with all its splendour and glory. It was the Star of Bethlehem. I could now say in the language of the poet—

> 'Once on the raging seas I rode,
>   The storm was loud, the night was dark;
> The ocean yawned, and rudely blowed
>   The wind that tossed my foundering bark.'

Yes, I hope to sing some day in the realms of bliss—

> 'It was my guide, my light, my all!
> It bade my dark foreboding cease;
> And through the storm and danger's thrall,
> It led me to the port of peace.'

I have not the happiness of being able to refer to written records in narrating the history of my forefathers; but I can reveal to the world what has long been laid up in my memory; so that when 'I go the way of all the earth', the crooked and singular paths which I have made in the world, may not only be a warning to others, but may inspire them with a trust in God. And not only a warning and a trust, but also that the world may learn that there once lived such a man as Kah-ge-ga-gah-bowh, when they read his griefs and his joys.

My parents were of the Ojebwa nation, who lived on the lake back of Cobourg, on the shores of Lake Ontario, Canada West. The lake was called Rice Lake, where there was a quantity of wild rice, and much game of different kinds, before the whites cleared away the woods, where the deer and the bear then resorted.

My father and mother were taught the religion of their nation. My father became a medicine man in the early part of his life, and always had by him the implements of war, which generally distinguish our head men. He was a good hunter as any in the tribe. Very few brought more furs than he did in the spring. Every spring they returned from their hunting grounds. The Ojebwas each claimed, and claim to this day, hunting grounds, rivers, lakes, and whole districts of country. No one hunted on each other's ground. My father had the northern fork of the river Trent, above Bellmont Lake.

My great-grandfather was the first who ventured to settle at Rice Lake, after the Ojebwa nation defeated the Hurons, who once inhabited all the lakes in Western Canada, and who had a large village just on the top of the hill of the Anderson farm (which was afterwards occupied by the Ojebwas), and which furnished a magnificent view of the lakes and surrounding country. He was of the *Crane tribe*, i.e. had a crane for totem—*coat of arms*—which now forms the totem of the villagers, excepting those who have since come amongst us from other villages by intermarriage, for there was a law that no one was to marry one of the same totem, for all considered each other as being related. He must have been a daring adventurer—*a warrior*—for no one would have ventured to go and settle down on the land from which they had just driven the Hurons, whom the Ojebwas conquered and reduced, unless he was a great hero. It is said that he lived about the islands of Rice Lake, secreting himself from the enemy for several years, until some others came and joined him, when they formed a settlement on one of the islands. He must have been a great hunter, for this was one of the principal inducements that made him venture there, for there must have been abundance of game of every kind. The Ojebwas are called, here and all around, Massisuagays, because they came from Me-sey Sah-gieng, at the head of Lake Huron, as you go up to Sault St. Marie falls.

Here he lived in jeopardy—with his life in his hand—enduring the unpleasant idea that he lived in the land of bones—*amidst the gloom*, which shrouded the once happy and populous village of the Hurons; here their bones lay broadcast around his wigwam; where, among these woods once rang the war cry of the Hurons, echoing along the valley of the river Trent, but whose sinewed arms now laid low, with their badges and arms of war, in one common grave, near the residence of Peter Anderson, Esq. Their graves, forming a hillock, are now all that remain of this once powerful nation. Their bones, gun barrels, tomahawks, war spears, large scalping knives, are yet to be found there. This must have taken place soon after the formation of the settlement in Quebec.

The *Crane tribe* became the sole proprietors of this part of the Ojebwa land; the descendants of this tribe will continue to wear the distinguishing sign; except in a few instances, the chiefs are of this tribe.

My grandfather lived here about this time, and held some friendly intercourse with the whites. My father here learned the manners, customs, and worship of the nation. He, and others, became acquainted with the early settlers, and have ever been friendly with the whites. And I know the day when he used to shake the hand of the white man, and, *very friendly*, the white man would say, '*take some whiskey.*' When he saw any hungering for venison, he gave them to eat; and some, in return for his kindness, have repaid him after they became good and great farmers.

My mother was of the *Eagle tribe*; she was a sensible woman; she was as good a hunter as any of the Indians; she could shoot the deer, and the ducks flying, as well as they. Nature had done a great deal for her, for she was active; and she was much more cleanly than the majority of our women in those days. She lived to see the day when most of her children were given up to the Lord in Christian baptism; while she experienced a change of heart, and the fullness of God in man, for she lived daily in the enjoyment of God's favours. I will speak more of her at a proper time, respecting her life and happy death.

My father still lives; he is from sixty-five to seventy years old, and is one of the chiefs of Rice Lake Indian Village. He used to love fire-water before he was converted to God, but now lives in the enjoyment of religion, and he is happy without the devil's spittal—*whiskey*. If Christianity had not come, and the grace of God had not taken possession of his heart, his head would soon have been laid low beneath the fallen leaves of the forest, and I, left, in my youthful days, an orphan. But to God be all the praise for his timely deliverance.

The reader will see that I cannot boast of an exalted parentage, nor trace the past history to some renowned warrior in days of yore; but let the above suffice. My fathers were those who endured much; who first took possession of the conquered lands of the Hurons.

I was born in *nature's wide domain!* The trees were all that sheltered my infant limbs—the blue heavens all that covered me. I am one of Nature's children; I have always admired her; she shall be my glory; her features—her robes, and the wreath about her brow—the seasons—her stately oaks, and the evergreen—her hair—ringlets over the earth, all contribute to my enduring love of her; and wherever I see her, emotions of pleasure roll in my breast, and swell and burst like waves on the shores of the ocean, in prayer and praise to Him who has placed me in her hand. It is thought great to be born in palaces, surrounded with wealth—but to be born in nature's wide domain is greater still!

I was born sometime in the fall of 1818, near the mouth of the river Trent, called in our language, Sah-ge-dah-we-ge-wah-noong, while my father and mother were attending the annual distribution of the presents from the government to the Indians. I was the third of our family; a brother and sister being older, both of whom died. My brother died without the knowledge of the Saviour, but my sister experienced the power of the loving grace of God. One brother, and two step-brothers, are still alive.

I remember the tall trees, and the dark woods—the swamp just by, where the little wren sang so melodiously after the going down of the sun in the west—the current of the broad river Trent—the skipping of the fish, and the noise of the rapids a little above. It was here I first saw the light; a little fallen down shelter, made of evergreens, and a few dead embers, the remains of the last fire that shed its genial warmth around, were all that marked the spot. When I last visited it, nothing but four poles stuck in the ground, and they were leaning on account of decay. Is this dear spot, made green by the tears of memory, any less enticing and hallowed than the palaces where princes are born? I would much more glory in this birth-place, with the broad canopy of heaven above me, and the giant arms of the forest trees for my shelter, than to be born in palaces of marble, studded with pillars of gold! Nature will be nature still, while palaces shall decay and fall in ruins. Yes, Niagara will be Niagara a thousand years hence! The rainbow, a wreath over her brow, shall continue as long as the sun, and the flowing of the river! While the work of art, however impregnable, shall in atoms fall.

Our wigwam we always carried with us wherever we went. It was made in the following manner: Poles were cut about fifteen feet long; three with crotches at the end, which were stuck in the ground some distance apart, the upper ends meeting, and fastened with bark; and then other poles were cut in circular form and bound round the first, and then covered with plaited reeds, or sewed birch bark, leaving an opening on top for the smoke to escape. The skins of animals formed a covering for a gap, which answered for a door. The family all seated tailor-fashion on mats. In the fall and winter they were generally made more secure, for the purpose of keeping out the rain and cold. The covering of our wigwam was always carried by my mother, whenever we went through the woods. In the summer it was easier and pleasanter to move about from place to place, than in the winter. In the summer we had birch bark canoes, and with these we travelled very rapidly and easily. In the winter everything was carried upon the back. I have known some Indians to carry a whole deer—not a small one, but a buck. If an Indian could lift up his pack off the ground by means of his arms, it was a good load, not too light nor too heavy. I once carried one hundred and ninety-six weight of flour, twelve pounds of shot, five pounds of coffee, and some sugar, about a quarter of a mile, without resting—the flour was in two bags. It felt very heavy. This was since I travelled with the missionaries, in going over one of the portages in the west.

Our summer houses were made like those in gardens among the whites, except that the skeleton is covered with bark.

The hunting grounds of the Indians were secured by right, a law and custom among themselves. No one was allowed to hunt on another's land, without invitation or permission. If any person was found trespassing on the ground of another, all his things were taken from him, except a handful of shot, powder sufficient to serve him in going *straight* home, a gun, a tomahawk, and a knife; all the fur, and other things, were taken from him. If he were found a second time trespassing, all his things were taken away from him, except food sufficient to subsist on while going home. And should he still come a third time to trespass on the same, or another man's hunting grounds, his nation, or tribe, are then informed of it, who take up his case. If still he disobey, he is banished from his tribe.

My father's hunting ground was at the head of Crow River, a branch of the River Trent, north of the Prince Edward District, Canada West. There are two branches to this river—one belongs to George Poudash, one of the principal chiefs of our nation; the other to my father; and the Crow River belongs to another chief by the name of John Crow. During the last war the Indians did not hunt or fish much for nearly six years, and at the end of that time there were large quantities of beaver, otter, minks, lynx, fishes, &c.

These hunting grounds abound with rivers and lakes; the face of the country is swampy and rocky; the deer and the bear abound in these woods; part of the surrendered territory is included in it. In the year 1818, 1,800,000 acres of it were surrendered to the British government. For how much, do you ask? For $2,690 per annum! What a *great sum* for British generosity!

Much of the back country still remains unsold, and I hope the scales will be removed from the eyes of my poor countrymen, that they may see the robberies perpetrated upon them, before they surrender another foot of territory.

From these lakes and rivers come the best furs that are caught in Western Canada. Buyers of fur get large quantities from here. They are then shipped to New York City, or to England. Whenever fruit is plenty, bears are also plenty, and there is much bear hunting. Before the whites came amongst us, the skins of these animals served for clothing; they are now sold from three to eight dollars apiece.

My father generally took one or two families with him when he went to hunt; all were to hunt, and place their gains into one common stock till spring, (for they were often out all winter,) when a division took place.

* * *

My beloved Reader—I am now about closing my narrative, and in doing this there are but a few things to say. Throughout the work, I have confined my remarks chiefly to my own nation. But it must not be supposed, on this account, that I am forgetful of my brethren of the other Indian nations. The prayers and benevolent efforts of all Christendom should be directed towards all men everywhere. The gospel should be preached to every creature; and the field is the *wide* WORLD.

The Menomenees in Wisconsin, the Winebagoes and Potawatamies in Iowa, the warlike nations of the Sacs and Foxes, the Osages, Pawnees, Mandans, Kansas, Creeks, Omahas, Otoes, Delawares, Iowas, and a number of others elsewhere, must perish as did their brethren in the Eastern States, unless the white man send them the Gospel, and the blessings of education. There is field enough for all denominations to labour in, without interfering with each other. It is too late in the day to assert that the Indians cannot be raised up out of their degraded state, and educated for God and heaven. None need be discouraged since the Ojebwas in Western Canada have been converted. No language is adequate to portray the misery, wretchedness, and degradation in which we were, when the word of God was first brought and preached to us.

It is not necessary to detail each and every wrong, that my poor people have suffered at the hands of the white man. Enough has already been said in various parts of the work, to prove that they have been most grossly abused, peeled, and wronged. Nor shall I notice the *personal wrongs* that I myself have received; and from those, too, of whom I had good reason to hope better things. I once thought, that there were some things that I could never forgive; but the religion of Jesus, and the law of love, have taught me differently. I *do* forgive them; and may God forgive them and me too.

I have sometimes heard it said, that our forefathers were cruel to the forefathers of the whites. But was not this done through ignorance, or in self-defence? Had your fathers adopted the plan of the great philanthropist, William Penn, neither fields, nor clubs, nor waters, would have been crimsoned with each other's blood. The white men have been like the greedy lion, pouncing upon and devouring its prey. They have driven us from our nation, our homes, and possessions; compelled us to seek a refuge in Missouri, among strangers, and wild beasts; and will, perhaps, soon compel us to scale the Rocky Mountains; and, for aught I can tell, we may yet be driven to the Pacific Ocean, there to find our graves. My only trust is, that there is a just God. Was it to perpetrate such acts that you have been exalted above all other nations? Providence intended you for a *blessing* and not a *curse* to us. You have sent your missionaries to Burmah, China, the Sandwich Islands, and to almost every part of the world; and shall the Indians *perish at your own door*?

Is it not well known that the Indians have a generous and magnanimous heart? I feel proud to mention in this connection, the names of a Pocahontas, Massasoit, Skenandoah, Logan, Kusic, Pushmataha, Philip, Tecumseh, Osceola, Petalesharro, and thousands of others. Such names are an honour to the world! Let a late Governor of Massachusetts* speak for our fathers, when they first beheld the trembling white man:—

'Brothers! when our fathers came over the great waters, they were a small band. The red man stood upon the rock by the seaside, and saw our fathers. He might have pushed them into the water and drowned them. But he stretched out his arms to our fathers and said, "Welcome, white men!" Our fathers were hungry, and the red man gave them corn and venison. Our fathers were cold, and the red man wrapped them up in his blanket. We are now numerous and powerful, but we remember the kindness of the red man to our fathers.'

---

* Edward Everett, Esq.

And what have we received since, in return? Is it for the deeds of a Pocahontas, a Massasoit, and a host of others, that we have been plundered and oppressed, and expelled from the hallowed graves of our ancestors? If help cannot be obtained from England and America, where else can we look? Will you then, lend us a helping hand; and make some amends for past injuries?

It is often said, that the Indians are revengeful, cruel, and ungovernable. But go to them with nothing but the Bible in your hands, and Love in your hearts, and you may live with them in perfect safety, share their morsel with them, and, like the celebrated Bartram, return to your homes unharmed. They very soon learn to venerate the Bible; as a proof of this, I will give an instance, that came under my own eye:—While at the Rabbit River Mission, a chief from the west, visited me. After reading to him several chapters from the Bible, he said, with much surprise, 'Is this the book, that I hear so much about in my country?' I replied, yes; and these are the words of Ke-sha-mon-e-doo (the Great Spirit). 'Will you not,' said he, 'give me one? I wish to show it to my people.' I told him, not without you first promise that you will take care of it. He promised me that he would. I handed it to him; he took it, and turned it over and over, and then exclaimed, 'Wonderful, wonderful! This is the book of the Great Spirit! ' He then wrapped it up in a silk handkerchief, and the handkerchief in three or four folds of cloth. I heard, afterwards, from the trader, that the book was still kept sacred. O, if my poor brother could but read and understand that blessed volume, how soon would his dumb idols be 'cast down to the moles and to the bats'! Will no one go and tell him and his nation, of the boundless, beseeching, bleeding, dying love of a Saviour; and urge upon them the importance of such a preparation of heart, as will enable them 'to give up their account with joy'? The Great Spirit is no respecter of persons; He has made of one blood all the nations of the earth; He loves all his children alike; and his highest attributes are love, mercy, and justice. If this be so,—and who dare doubt it?—will He not stretch out his hand and help them, and avenge their wrongs? 'If offences must come', let it be recollected, that woe is denounced against them 'from whom they come'.

I again propose that the territories of the Indians, in the British dominions, be annexed to that Government, and those in the American dominions to the Federal Union. And, finally, in the language of that excellent, magnanimous, and benevolent friend of the poor children of the forest, Col. Thomas McKenney, I would say,

'I have already referred, in the commencement of this proposal to annex the Indian territory to our Union, to those good men, who, in the character of missionaries, have kept side by side with the Indians in so many of their afflictions and migrations. I will again refer to them, and implore them by all the lost labour of the past, and by the hopes of the future; by the critical condition of the pacific relations that exist between the Indians and us; and by the sacredness of the cause in which they are engaged, to look well and earnestly into this subject, and learn from the past what *must* attend upon their labours in the future, if the change I propose, or some other change equivalent to it, be not brought about. And, seeing, as they must see, that the plan I propose, or some other, is indispensable to the success they seek to command, I implore them to take up the subject in all its bearings, and by the instrumentalities which they have at command, manufacture, collect, and embody public opinion, in regard to what may be determined to be done; and by memorial, and personal agencies, bring this opinion to bear upon Congress, with whom alone the power is vested, to redeem, disenthrall, and save, and bless, the remnants of this aboriginal race. And I make the same appeal to all the good, of all religious persuasions, both in the Church and out of it, and politicians of all parties, to second this attempt, feeble as I know it to be, to save the Indians, and consolidate, and perpetuate peace between them and us, and, by so doing, ward off the terrible retribution which must sooner or later, unless it be averted, fall upon this nation.'

[1847]

Catherine Soneegoh Sutton
1822–1865

Mississauga Anishinaabe

Catherine Soneegoh Sutton, whose Ojibwe name was Nah-nee-bah-wee-quay ('Upright Woman'), was born near the Credit River in present-day Ontario. When she was two, her family moved to the Credit Indian village, a Methodist settlement. In 1837 she went to England with her aunt, who was the wife of Peter Jones, the first Indigenous Canadian to be ordained.

After attending school in England for a year, Sutton returned to Canada and in 1839 married an English immigrant, William Sutton. Together they served as Methodist missionaries in various venues, including a model farm near Sault Ste Marie in 1852 and a mission in Michigan two years later. The Nawash band of Owen Sound had ceded them land in 1845, but when they returned to Owen Sound in 1857 the land had been laid out for sale. Sutton was first refused a share of the Nawash band's annuities for having married a white man and for having being absent from the country, and then was not allowed to purchase the land because she was an Indian. By giving a series of lectures in Canada and the United States, Sutton was able to raise money for a journey to England, where she petitioned the Queen. As a result, she was able to return to Canada and buy back some of the land. She continued actively to pursue Indigenous rights until her death in 1865.

The following selection is from an entry in her journal, which is held in the Grey County and Owen Sound Museum. It is taken here from *Native Literature in Canada* (1990), by Penny Petrone, who surmises that it is a copy of a letter written in response to an editorial in the periodical *The Leader*. The entry is dated 8 September 1864.

Letter

On the shores of Goulais Bay Lake Superior and the neighbouring one of Batchawana, one of these publick nusiances—an Indian reserve was laid of a few years ago under Lord Elgin's Government the reserve covered a portage

In His Father's Village, Someone Was Just About to Go Out Hunting Birds | 27

Going through the pines, 5
just to where the ponds lay,
he heard geese calling.
Then he went in that direction.

There were two women bathing in a lake.
Something lay there on the shore. 10
Two goose skins were thrown over it.
Under their tails were patches of white.

After watching for a while,
he swooped in.
He sat on the two skins. 15
The women asked to have them back.

He asked the better-looking one to marry him.
The other one replied.
'Don't marry my younger sister.
I am smarter. Marry me.' 20

'No. I will marry your younger sister.'

And she said that she accepted him, they say.

'Well then! Marry my younger sister.
You caught us bathing in a lake
that belongs to our father. 25
Now give me my skin.'

He gave it back.
She slipped it on
while she was swimming in the lake.

A goose swam in the lake then, 30
and then she started calling.
And then she flew, they say,
though leaving her younger sister
sickened her heart.

She circled above them. 35
Then she flew off, they say.
She passed through the sky.

He gave the younger woman one of his marten-skin blankets,
and he brought her home, they say.

A two-headed redcedar stood at the edge of the village, 40
and he put his wife's skin between the trunks.
Then he brought her into his father's house.

The headman's son had taken a wife.
So his father invited the people, they say.
They offered her food. 45
She did nothing but smell it.
She would eat no human food.

Later, her husband's mother started steaming silverweed, they say.
Then she paid closer attention.
When her husband's mother was still busy cooking, 50
she asked her husband
to ask her to hurry, they say.

They placed it before her.
It vanished.
And then they began to feed her this only, they say. 55

After a time, as he was sleeping,
his wife lay down beside him, and her skin was cold.
When it happened again,
he decided to watch her, they say.

He lay still in the bed, 60
and he felt her moving away from him slowly, they say.
Then she went out.
He followed behind her.

She walked along the beach in front of the village.
She went where the skin was kept. 65
From there, she flew.
She landed beyond the point at the edge of town.

He started toward her.
She was eating the eelgrass that grew there,
and the breaking waves were lifting her back toward shore. 70
He saw her, they say.
And then she flew back where they kept her skin.

There in the house, he asked them, they say,
'Who will carry my son-in-law back?'

And a loon said,
'I will carry your son-in-law back.' 275

'How will you do it?' he asked.

The loon said,
'I will put him under my tail
and dive right in front here.
Then I'll come up again at the edge of his father's town 280
and release him.'

They thought he was too weak to do it, they say.

His father-in-law asked the question again.
A grebe gave the same reply.
They thought she was also too weak. 285

And a raven said he would carry him back.
And they asked him, 'How will you do it?'

'I will put him under my wing
and fly with him from the edge of the village.
When I'm tired, 290
I'll let myself tumble and fall with him.'

They were pleased with his answer, they say,
and they all came down to the edge of the village to watch.

He did as he said.
When he grew tired, 295
he let himself fall down through the clouds with him
and dropped him onto a shoal exposed by the tide.

'Hwuuu! What a load I have carried.'

Becoming a gull, he squawked and went on squawking.

This is where it ends. 300

[1900]

E. Pauline Johnson 1861–1913

Mohawk

Pauline Johnson's place in Canadian literature has always been political. Emily Pauline Johnson, Tekahionwake, was born on the Six Nations Reserve at a time when Canadian culture was mainly imperialist. As the daughter of a Mohawk chief, George Henry Martin Johnson, and his English wife, Emily Susanna Howells, her family connections established her as both Indigenous aristocracy and Loyalist descendant. Her pro-British proclamations continued the allegiance of her illustrious ancestors, such as her grandfather, John Smoke Johnson, a hero of the War of 1812. Johnson originally performed only as a means of supporting her poetry, but she became one of Canada's most prominent recitalists. She was an ethereal, enigmatic, and romantic figure in her stage persona as both the Indian princess and the Victorian genteel lady. Johnson, usually appearing in buckskin and beads for the first half of her recital, employed the theatrical aid of a mesmerizing costume, which contrasted highly to the formal evening gown that she wore for the second half of her performance. The oral traditions gave her the status of a bard or orator, and Johnson recited her poetry with dramatic gestures. Johnson's poetry covers a range of subjects but focuses largely on the patriotic or pastoral 'Indian'. Almost all are short lyrics and narratives. Her short prose narratives often have a moral direction, often referring to the character and treatment of Indigenous peoples.

Johnson's work combines genre writing, with all of its popular appeal, with substantial comments on the position of Indigenous peoples in her society. This combination causes A. LaVonne Brown Ruoff to consider Johnson a late but typical example of the Victorian woman writer. Johnson's adventure stories, many of which are collected in *The Shagganappi* (1913), demonstrate a clear moral agenda. In their publication in *The Boy's World*, a prominent American example of 'muscular Christianity', they provide a constant recitation of the moral character of Indigenous peoples and, in particular, their civilization. Johnson's poetry and stories for other periodicals from the period, such as *Mother's Magazine*, show that she grasped the didactic potential of her venue and produced material that is, as Ruoff notes, both pro-Indigenous and feminist. Although complicated by works such as 'Canadian Born', the title poem of her second collection of poetry, Johnson always possessed clear perceptions of her racial position as indicated in such pivotal work as 'A Cry from an Indian Wife' and 'The Cattle Thief'. In his introduction to *The Shagganappi*, Ernest Thompson Seton quotes her: 'There are those who think they pay me a compliment in saying that I am just like a white woman. My aim, my joy, my pride is to sing the glories of my own people.' Another quotation chosen by Seton shows Johnson's romantic histrionics but also her recognition of her symbolic position:

> Oh, why have our people forced on me the name of Pauline Johnson? Was not my Indian name good enough? Do you think you help us by bidding us to forget our blood? by teaching us to cast off all memory of our high ideals and our glorious past? I am an Indian. My pen and my life I devote to the memory of my own people. Forget that I was Pauline Johnson, but remember always that I was Tekahionwake, the Mohawk that humbly aspired to be the saga singer of her people, the bard of the

noblest folk the world has ever seen, the sad historian of her own heroic race.

Johnson used the 'noble savage' archetype implied by the words 'saga singer' and 'bard' to argue against the racist assumption of the dying Indigenous society, which 'sad historian' implies, and to create a space in popular literature for Indigenous issues presented from a specifically Indigenous perspective. While living on the west coast towards the end of her short life, Johnson's emphasis on the Indigenous tradition and perspective was further illustrated in *Legends of Vancouver* (1911), a collection of mythic narratives as told by Chief Capilano.

Neglected initially by the Canadian literary establishment, Johnson's achievements have now begun to be recognized, as shown by the biography *Paddling Her Own Canoe: The Times and Texts of E. Pauline Johnson (Tekahionwake)* (2000) by Veronica Stong-Boag and Carole Gerson, and by the collection they edited, *E. Pauline Johnson, Tekahionwake: Collected Poems and Selected Prose* (2002). In the latter, particular attention should be paid to 'A Strong Race Opinion: On the Indian Girl in Modern Fiction,' which offers an analysis of the stereotype that is well in advance of her contemporaries. The aforementioned poems included in this edition provide concrete examples of the kind of representation Johnson's advocated for, in featuring strong Indigenous women who challenge both stereotypes and patriarchy.

A Cry from an Indian Wife

My forest brave, my Red-skin love, farewell;
We may not meet to-morrow; who can tell
What mighty ills befall our little band,
Or what you'll suffer from the white man's hand?

Here is your knife! I thought 'twas sheathed for aye.　　　5
No roaming bison calls for it to-day;
No hide of prairie cattle will it maim;
The plains are bare, it seeks a nobler game:

'Twill drink the life-blood of a soldier host.
Go; rise and strike, no matter what the cost.　　　10
Yet stay. Revolt not at the Union Jack,
Nor raise Thy hand against this stripling pack
Of white-faced warriors, marching West to quell
Our fallen tribe that rises to rebel.
They all are young and beautiful and good;　　　15
Curse to the war that drinks their harmless blood.
Curse to the fate that brought them from the East
To be our chiefs—to make our nation least
That breathes the air of this vast continent.
Still their new rule and council is well meant.　　　20
They but forget we Indians owned the land

From ocean unto ocean; that they stand
Upon a soil that centuries agone
Was our sole kingdom and our right alone.
They never think how they would feel to-day,   25
If some great nation came from far away,
Wresting their country from their hapless braves,
Giving what they gave us—but wars and graves.
Then go and strike for liberty and life,
And bring back honour to your Indian wife.   30
Your wife? Ah, what of that, who cares for me?
Who pities my poor love and agony?
What white-robed priest prays for your safety here,
As prayer is said for every volunteer
That swells the ranks that Canada sends out?   35
Who prays for vict'ry for the Indian scout?
Who prays for our poor nation lying low?
None—therefore take your tomahawk and go.
My heart may break and burn into its core,
But I am strong to bid you go to war.   40
Yet stay, my heart is not the only one
That grieves the loss of husband and of son;
Think of the mothers o'er the inland seas;
Think of the pale-faced maiden on her knees;
One pleads her God to guard some sweet-faced child   45
That marches on toward the North-West wild.
The other prays to shield her love from harm,
To strengthen his young, proud uplifted arm.
Ah, how her white face quivers thus to think,
Your tomahawk his life's best blood will drink.   50
She never thinks of my wild aching breast,
Nor prays for your dark face and eagle crest
Endangered by a thousand rifle balls,
My heart the target if my warrior falls.
O! coward self I hesitate no more;   55
Go forth, and win the glories of the war.
Go forth, nor bend to greed of white men's hands,
By right, by birth we Indians own these lands,
Though starved, crushed, plundered, lies our nation low . . .
Perhaps the white man's God has willed it so.   65

[1885]

Shadow River

Muskoka

A stream of tender gladness,
Of filmy sun, and opal tinted skies;
Of warm midsummer air that lightly lies
In mystic rings,
Where softly swings   5
The music of a thousand wings
That almost tones to sadness.

Midway 'twixt earth and heaven,
A bubble in the pearly air, I seem
To float upon the sapphire floor, a dream   10
Of clouds of snow,
Above, below,
Drift with my drifting, dim and slow,
As twilight drifts to even.

The little fern-leaf, bending   15
Upon the brink, its green reflection greets,
And kisses soft the shadow that it meets
With touch so fine,
The border line
The keenest vision can't define;   20
So perfect is the blending.

The far, fir trees that cover
The brownish hills with needles green and gold,
The arching elms o'erhead, vinegrown and old,
Repictured are   25
Beneath me far,
Where not a ripple moves to mar
Shades underneath, or over.

Mine is the undertone;
The beauty, strength, and power of the land   30
Will never stir or bend at my command;
But all the shade
Is marred or made,

If I but dip my paddle blade;
And it is mine alone, 35

O! pathless world of seeming!
O! pathless life of mine whose deep ideal
Is more my own than ever was the real.
For others Fame
And Love's red flame, 40
And yellow gold; I only claim
The shadows and the dreaming.

[1889]

The Song My Paddle Sings

West wind, blow from your prairie nest,
Blow from the mountains, blow from the west.
The sail is idle, the sailor too;
O! wind of the west, we wait for you.
Blow, blow! 5
I have wooed you so,
But never a favour you bestow.
You rock your cradle the hills between,
But scorn to notice my white lateen.

I stow the sail, unship the mast: 10
I wooed you long but my wooing's past;
My paddle will lull you into rest.
O! drowsy wind of the drowsy west,
Sleep, sleep,
By your mountain steep, 15
Or down where the prairie grasses sweep!
Now fold in slumber your laggard wings,
For soft is the song my paddle sings.

August is laughing across the sky,
Laughing while paddle, canoe and I, 20
Drift, drift,
Where the hills uplift
On either side of the current swift.

The river rolls in its rocky bed;
My paddle is plying its way ahead; 25

Dip, dip,
While the waters flip
In foam as over their breast we slip.

And oh, the river runs swifter now;
The eddies circle about my bow. 30
Swirl, swirl!
How the ripples curl
In many a dangerous pool awhirl!

And forward far the rapids roar,
Fretting their margin for evermore. 35
Dash, dash,
With a mighty crash,
They seethe, and boil, and bound, and splash.

Be strong, O paddle! be brave, canoe!
The reckless waves you must plunge into. 40
Reel, reel,
On your trembling keel,
But never a fear my craft will feel.

We've raced the rapid, we're far ahead!
The river slips through its silent bed. 45
Sway, sway,
As the bubbles spray
And fall in tinkling tunes away.

And up on the hills against the sky,
A fir tree rocking its lullaby, 50
Swings, swings,
Its emerald wings,
Swelling the song that my paddle sings.

[1892]

The Cattle Thief

They were coming across the prairie, they were galloping hard and fast;
For the eyes of those desperate riders had sighted their man at last—
Sighted him off to Eastward, where the Cree encampment lay,
Where the cotton woods fringed the river, miles and miles away.

Mistake him? Never! Mistake him? the famous Eagle Chief! 5
That terror to all the settlers, that desperate Cattle Thief—
That monstrous, fearless Indian, who lorded it over the plain,
Who thieved and raided, and scouted, who rode like a hurricane!
But they've tracked him across the prairie; they've followed him hard and fast;
For those desperate English settlers have sighted their man at last. 10

Up they wheeled to the tepees, all their British blood aflame,
Bent on bullets and bloodshed, bent on bringing down their game;
But they searched in vain for the Cattle Thief: that lion had left his lair,
And they cursed like a troop of demons—for the women alone were there
'The sneaking Indian coward,' they hissed; 'he hides while yet he can; 15
He'll come in the night for cattle, but he's scared to face a *man*.'
'Never!' and up from the cotton woods rang the voice of Eagle Chief;
And right out into the open stepped, unarmed, the Cattle Thief.
Was that the game they had coveted? Scarce fifty years had rolled
Over that fleshless, hungry frame, starved to the bone and old; 20
Over that wrinkled, tawny skin, unfed by the warmth of blood.
Over those hungry, hollow eyes that glared for the sight of food.

He turned, like a hunted lion: 'I know not fear,' said he;
And the words outleapt from his shrunken lips in the language of the Cree.
'I'll fight you, white-skins, one by one, till I kill you *all*,' he said; 25
But the threat was scarcely uttered, ere a dozen balls of lead
Whizzed through the air about him like a shower of metal rain,
And the gaunt old Indian Cattle Thief dropped dead on the open plain.
And that band of cursing settlers gave one triumphant yell,
And rushed like a pack of demons on the body that writhed and fell. 30
'Cut the fiend up into inches, throw his carcass on the plain;
Let the wolves eat the cursed Indian, he'd have treated us the same.'
A dozen hands responded, a dozen knives gleamed high,
But the first stroke was arrested by a woman's strange, wild cry.
And out into the open, with a courage past belief, 35
She dashed, and spread her blanket o'er the corpse of the Cattle Thief;
And the words outleapt from her shrunken lips in the language of the Cree,
'If you mean to touch that body, you must cut your way through *me*.'
And that band of cursing settlers dropped backward one by one,
For they knew that an Indian woman roused, was a woman to let alone. 40
And then she raved in a frenzy that they scarcely understood,
Raved of the wrongs she had suffered since her earliest babyhood:
'Stand back, stand back, you white-skins, touch that dead man to your shame;
You have stolen my father's spirit, but his body I only claim.

You have killed him, but you shall not dare to touch him now he's dead.   45
You have cursed, and called him a Cattle Thief, though you robbed him
    first of bread—
Robbed him and robbed my people—look there, at that shrunken face,
Starved with a hollow hunger, we owe to you and your race.
What have you left to us of land, what have you left of game,
What have you brought but evil, and curses since you came?   50
How have you paid us for our game? how paid us for our land?
By a *book*, to save our souls from the sins *you* brought in your other hand.
Go back with your new religion, we never have understood
Your robbing an Indian's *body*, and mocking his *soul* with food.
Go back with your new religion, and find—if find you can—   55
The *honest* man you have ever made from out a *starving* man.
You say your cattle are not ours, your meat is not our meat;
When *you* pay for the land you live in, *we'll* pay for the meat we eat.
Give back our land and our country, give back our herds of game;
Give back the furs and the forests that were ours before you came;   60
Give back the peace and the plenty. Then come with your new belief,
And blame, if you dare, the hunger that *drove* him to be a thief.'

[1894]

The Corn Husker

Hard by the Indian lodges, where the bush
    Breaks in a clearing, through ill-fashioned fields,
She comes to labour, when the first still hush
    Of autumn follows large and recent yields.

Age in her fingers, hunger in her face,   5
    Her shoulders stooped with weight of work and years,
But rich in tawny colouring of her race,
    She comes a-field to strip the purple ears.

And all her thoughts are with the days gone by,
    Ere might's injustice banished from their lands   10
Her people, that to-day unheeded lie,
    Like the dead husks that rustle through her hands.

[1896]

Canadian Born

We first saw light in Canada, the land beloved of God;
We are the pulse of Canada, its marrow and its blood:
And we, the men of Canada, can face the world and brag
That we were born in Canada beneath the British flag.

Few of us have the blood of kings, few are of courtly birth, 5
But few are vagabonds or rogues of doubtful name and worth;
And all have one credential that entitles us to brag—
That we were born in Canada beneath the British flag.

We've yet to make our money, we've yet to make our fame,
But we have gold and glory in our clean colonial name; 10
And every man's a millionaire if only he can brag
That he was born in Canada beneath the British flag.

No title and no coronet is half so proudly worn
As that which we inherited as men Canadian born.
We count no man so noble as the one who makes the brag 15
That he was born in Canada beneath the British flag.

The Dutch may have their Holland, the Spaniard have his Spain,
The Yankee to the south of us must south of us remain;
For not a man dare lift a hand against the men who brag
That they were born in Canada beneath the British flag. 20

[1897]

Mary Augusta Tappage
1888–c. 1978

Shuswap

Mary Augusta Tappage, known to her community as Augusta, was born at Soda Creek in British Columbia's Cariboo country, 11 February 1888. Her background was Shuswap and Métis. At the age of four, she was sent to a Catholic mission school near Williams Lake. Her memories of that period are typical of students from residential schools:

If we were heard speaking Shuswap, we were punished. We were made to write on the board one hundred times, 'I will not speak Indian any more.' . . . And now we are supposed to remember our language and our skills because they are almost lost. Well, they're going to be hard to get back because the new generations are not that interested.

Augusta left school at thirteen and returned to the reservation at Soda Creek. In 1903 she married George Evans, a non-status Shuswap, and so she lost her own Indian status. Augusta's working life was spent homesteading and subsistence farming on Deep Creek, near her birthplace. The education of her sons reflects her non-status position:

> My two boys, Joseph and George, they never went to school. Taxpayers' children couldn't go to the Mission. Well, I didn't care about that. But there was no other school close by, so I taught them myself. Yes, I guess they can read and reckon as good as most folk can. I taught them myself.

After the deaths of her husband and eldest son, Augusta worked cooking and cleaning for various families. She acted as informal foster mother to many young people. Like many other Indigenous people of her generation, Augusta committed great energy to cultural education, to keep Shuswap, which is not a written language, alive.

Tyee—Big Chief

Tyee Lake was called after big chief—it means big chief.
But *Tyee* is not Shuswap.
It's Chinook, I think.
But it's not my language.

Pashish'kwa—that means lake in my language.　　　　　　5
Shadad'kwa—that means river.

I can't tell you how to spell it.
But that's how we say it.
It's a hard language, Shuswap—real hard.

When I got out of Mission school　　　　　　10
I had to ask what the Indians were saying.
I couldn't understand them.
We were only allowed to speak English at school.
I almost forgot my own language.
It's Shuswap, my language.　　　　　　15

[1973]

The Lillooets

That was a big cloud of dust 'way down
to the south in the spring, yes.
It was the Lillooet Indians coming north,
coming north to the goldfields
up by Barkerville.　　　　　　5

They go north into that country to work,
to work all the time, hard,
horses and wagons, women and children,
and dogs, hiyu dogs, all going
up by Barkerville.   10

They work from the time they get there
till fall, till the leaves drop, yes,
and the snow comes and it freezes
the lakes and the creeks
up by Barkerville.   15

It was the Lillooets going by in the spring
with packing horses, packing freight, yes,
into the mines somewhere in the mountains
and into the creeks
up by Barkerville.   20

All from Lillooet and I see them passing,
They are passing and passing and, no,
I couldn't ask them where they go—
they speak a different language,
but they go up by Barkerville.   25

We speak Shuswap, all of us Shuswap—
Soda Creek, Sugar Cane, Alkali, Canoe Creek,
Dog Creek, Canim Lake—all speak Shuswap,
except the Lillooets who go
up by Barkerville.   30

They come back in the fall, these Lillooets,
tired, I guess, but lots of money, lots of fish,
not minding snow or mud. They laugh
thinking of summer, yes,
up by Barkerville.   35

[1973]

Christmas at the Mission

I remember Christmas at the Mission.
Always we used to have midnight mass.

But we didn't know about Christmas and holidays
Until the Sisters came.
The Sisters came from France, you know, 5
And they brought Christmas with them.

They were the Sisters of Infant Jesus,
Those who came.

The teachers who had been teaching us before,
They didn't bother or care 10
Or hold Christmas. When the Sisters came
Was when we first knew Christmas!

The Sisters made us a Christmas concert, taught us
To sing hymns and songs,
Say recitations to everybody, helped us 15
Decorate our first Christmas tree.

I can't tell you how beautiful that first Christmas tree!
Everything was changed!

And our shoe, our right shoe, had to be polished
And put up on a bench 20
On Christmas Eve for holding candies, yes,
And whatever present you were going to get.

And then we all went to chapel through the snow
That first Christmas for midnight mass.

[1973]

At Birth

I used to help at times of birth, yes,
I used to help all the women around here.
I learned it from my book, my blue doctor's book.
I used to read it all the time.

I made up my mind that if she needs help, 5
I will help her. I'm not scared.
You've got to be awfully quick. There's two lives there.
The baby and the mother.

Yes, two lives, and what you got to do it with
Those days? You've got to be quick   10
To cut the cord, keep the bed clean, take out
The afterbirth, discard it, burn it.

Yes, you've got to be quick, fix the baby,
Tie its navel so it will not bleed
To death—cut it about that long.   15
When it heals there's nothing left, you know.

Then you bandage the mother, pin her up,
Keep her clean, keep her in bed ten days.
The doctor told us this—but if I leave,
I guess she got up.   20

I never had to spank a baby
To make him cry—they always cried.
They were always alive and healthy.
Yes, mother and baby, alive and healthy.

[1973]

Martin Martin 1889-1976

Inuit

Martin Martin, born at Oka in Labrador, is part of a very specific environment. The Labrador coast has been used by whites as fishing grounds for centuries. A few remained on the shore to become known as 'settlers'. The population has remained small, and devoted to its own traditional ways—trapping and fishing—thus giving rise to the Canadian anomaly of a longstanding, isolated, subsistence-based white population.

As a result, there has been intermarriage and a general intermingling between Inuit, white, and Innu and Naskapi for a long time. Although the identities of the cultures have remained separate, and although there has been significant racial tension at times, there has also been an acceptance of the rights of tenure of all these populations, often stated in opposition to newcomers, and specifically to Newfoundlanders and Québécois.

The following reminiscences are taken from the Labrador magazine *Them Days*, which contains a multitude of personal experience narratives from all of the cultures. In its accounts of mixed-race lives from this unusual 'melting pot', it provides insights unseen in the records of other Canadian areas. And like various magazines and newspapers that represent other Indigenous communities, it also shows the 'literary' responses from Indigenous cultures at a time when there was no literary culture that included them.

We, the Inuit, Are Changing

Translated by William Kalleo

We, the Inuit here in Labrador, right to this day still have the traditional ways of our forefathers. Right to this day we eat what our forefathers used to eat, food with no price tags on it, food created for us ever since the earth was created. People have different foods according to their land. This I was not aware of in the past. Some eat only what is grown in gardens, others eat whatever food they can get their hands on and we the Inuit people, have a different diet because we are people of a cold land. Because we are people of a cold land, wildlife is our main diet. Our forefathers were strong because nothing was scarce, everything was plentiful in those past years. We, the younger generation, think we are hungry but we are not because there is plenty of the white man's foods available for us to obtain at any time. We only are hungry for wildlife meat because some years are plentiful and some years there is none at all. This I have found.

Our forefathers' ancestors, which we have just heard of but not seen, taught our fathers how to share any kill made amongst their people. So my father taught me to share my kill as it was the traditional way. When I was a young man every time I went hunting and came back successful I invited the poor, the less fortunate, and the old Inuit to share my kill. After they had eaten they would joke around and tell stories of the past. When I heard these happy people I was aware that this was a blessing. I had made my fellow people happy through sharing. Our Creator had blessed me and I had carried on this blessing by sharing because this was meant to be. It is sad how this tradition is being forgotten. Young people now keep their kill to themselves. Some will give a little to those they wish to share with. I have said what I have seen and experienced and I am aware that this tradition is no longer practised. I hope this will be written down so that our children can be made aware of what used to take place in past years.

We have not lost all our traditions and culture yet. We have not lost our ability to hunt wildlife game. We know how to locate and hunt the game. Our young men still try to hunt in the traditional ways but they have difficulties because there is less game now. But our young Inuit have not given up trying their best to hunt for wildlife food. This we will never lose as long as there are Inuit in Labrador.

I am one hundred per cent pure Eskimo. I was never educated in the white society way because when I was a child this was not practised. Our school term lasted only six months and our main subject was studying the word of God. We had to memorize Bible verses and speak them out from memory while our teachers listened. The only time we were given a new verse was when we mastered the one before. Because of this teaching we, the elderly Inuit, can still speak out by heart many verses of the Bible, at least I always could. I don't know of my fellow elders but I'm sure they too can speak out what they memorized as children. In this generation our children have almost a whole year to learn and study but they are learning only the white society way. No wonder they have a better knowledge than we, the elderly. I am not happy that they are only being taught the white society system. I would be happy if they were taught first the word of God, then how to deal with life. I say this because I think our children don't know the true meaning of life because they refuse to hear the word of God, or are encouraged to do so. Our Inuit children are taught, I suppose, how to survive in white communities but not in the Inuit land. When learning the white society way was first introduced, or enforced, as a way of teaching our Inuit children, I strongly objected because I foresaw that in the future they would forget our Inuit language and also the word of God. I have said this because it is what I have wanted to say for ever so long. I was involved when teaching our children in the white society way was forced on us. I was out-voted when I suggested that our children be taught the word of God first and other subjects after. I had no power to alter what was being forced on our children, my objections were not considered important. Now, what I tried to bring to attention, about our children losing their traditions and culture, is beginning to be realized by Inuit in different parts of Canada. All I have said is true. Our young Inuit have a complete new way of living and if it is let to continue, something will happen to show them they are leading a dangerous life.

In such a short time we, the Inuit of Labrador, have changed in many ways. We do not carry on many of our traditions. We are forced into many new ways which we do not even understand. Also in these days we have seen Inuit from other regions, those we had only heard about but we did not know if they had traditions and cultures which were similar to ours. Now, we see them in the flesh and see that our fellow Inuit share our traditions and culture.

Last March, when I reached the age of eighty-seven, I started to think that I had lived too long. Then another thought occurred to me, why am I still living when I am no longer able to live off the land and sea? Why am I still wandering among my fellow Inuit and being observed and told that I am no longer useful to my people? I thought once more, the Lord God has been merciful to me to this day because although I am an old man I still have a mouth which can give guidance to our younger Inuit. The years have taken their toll on me, on my hearing, my sight, and my ability to walk long distances. All are no longer good and I know why this is so. When I was a young man we used to hunt caribou in the different seasons. One spring we were returning from the land when the river trails were starting to get water on the ice. Early one morning, before the sun rose, we slid from the top of the country down to a lake. The river trail had frozen over during the night and so it was usable but as the sun rose the ice melted and we began to break through into the water. When our komatiks fell through we went over knee deep in the icy water to push and pull them out. We carried on all through the day, wading, pushing, and pulling our heavily laden komatiks. My legs became so numb that I could feel nothing. Ever since that time my legs are no longer good.

I wish you peace on earth. We may never see each other on earth but through God's will we will see each other in Heaven when we are removed from the earth. So, let us look forward to meeting each other where there will be no pain or sorrow but happiness and eternal life. I am an old man now. My name is Martin Martin. I wish all a happy and successful life.

[1974]

Alma Greene 1896-1984

Mohawk

Alma Greene, Gah-wonh-nos-doh ('Forbidden Voice'), was a Mohawk of the Turtle clan, a clan mother and a medicine woman who championed Longhouse traditions. She lived on the Grand River Lands of the Six Nations all her life. Greene's writing reveals her community's fraught history associated with colonialism and the political structures put in place to control Indigenous peoples. Throughout her life, Greene witnessed many changes—the loss of traditional longhouse governing structures, the loss of language, the pressure to assimilate—and she highlights the concerns she and many of her generation had for her people's future. As Greene indicates, although held in high esteem by some, Joseph Brant is nevertheless a controversial figure in his own community, and here she comments critically on his legacy:

I dreamed once that I went to the door of a longhouse here on the reserve. It was not, of course, the Mohawk longhouse, thanks to Joseph Brant. But it was one of the others where the Indians hold their own ceremonies.

When I got there the door would not open. I tried again and again, but it seemed as though something was pushing against it, holding it closed.

So I went around to the side, to a window, and looked in. There was the faithkeeper, crouched in horror in a corner. And the rest of the longhouse was filled with a serpent, as big around as a seven-inch pipe, lying from one end of the room to the other. That's one dream I think has already come true.

From 'A New Clan Mother',
Forbidden Voice

From *Forbidden Voice: Reflections of a Mohawk Indian*

Everything was starting to change.

Both Forbidden Voice's big brothers were married now, and the older one had taken over the farm. The younger one had always preferred his paycheck to the life of a farmer, so his father had settled him in a house on a lot elsewhere on the reservation and the son went off to work every day. Forbidden Voice's big sister had gone to the city. People shook their heads when they talked about her.

Even Sundays were different now. Sunday had always been a special day in their house, Sunday was extra good meals, Sunday was put away all your work, even the doll's clothes you had been sewing. Sunday was visitors, Methodist church in the morning, and the Anglican church in the afternoon, and in the evening the whole family into the parlour for father to read from the Bible that sat on the fall-leaf table with the red cloth.

Her father was a lay reader in the Anglican church, and the first English Forbidden Voice had ever heard was her father reading the Bible on Sundays. For a long time the reading was just a monotone to her. She couldn't make out any of the words and the tiresome noise seemed to go on and on forever. It wasn't at all like the liquid Mohawk tongue, or even the jerky syllables of the Cayugas. Later, when she heard white men speak it, English was always to sound loud and quarrelsome in her ear.

Now her father had left the church and, though she asked him, he wouldn't say why. One day she mentioned this to an old chief who knew about affairs on the reserve, and he said he could tell her why. He took her to his house and there he showed her a document, which was a copy of the Exchequer Court proceedings between the Six Nations and the New England Company.

The New England Company was a curious organization that had been formed in the seventeenth century for the express purpose of 'civilizing' the North American natives and propagating the gospel. The company had sent missionaries to the Grand Valley in the 1820s and they had built a school for the Mohawks that later came to be known as the Mohawk Institute. Now it seemed that these 'Christians' had sold the land they had got from the Indians, which to Forbidden Voice was the same as stealing it.

Forbidden Voice knew that many of her people believed the Christian missionaries had no right to try to make Indians change their own religion and way of worship. Didn't it say in the Bible, at the very beginning of Genesis, 'And God said, "Let us make man in Our own image, after Our likeness, and let them have dominion over the fish of the sea and over the fowl of the air". So God created men in His own image, in the image of God created He him male and female created He them'?

And wasn't it only later, in Chapter Five of Genesis, that God created Adam and Eve to inhabit the Garden of Eden in the old world? Surely this meant that Adam and Eve were created to inhabit a specific place in the old world and that the Indians were the original man-beings created in the new world, with the eternal right to hunt and fish for their food?

Hadn't Christ told his apostles when he sent them to teach and baptize in the old world, 'I have other sheep which are not of this fold; them I will gather in'? Surely this meant the Indians were Christ's special charges, and that all the popes and kings and bishops of the old world had no authority to interfere.

Forbidden Voice had seen with her very own eyes evidence that the Creator kept an eye on his special children. A tornado had swept through one summer causing death and destruction in its path. When it had started to get very dark on the reserve, and they could see the funnel-shaped cloud coming from the west, all the families had been called together. As they watched, the funnel cloud lifted high aloft and passed over their heads. When it had gone past Indian territory, they could see it come to earth again and go on its angry way. Didn't this mean the Creator was not displeased with the red men?

Her mother had taught her a prayer in Mohawk to repeat every night before she went to bed. All it said was 'God the Father, God the Son, God the Holy Ghost; Creator of the sun, the moon, the stars, and the earth. Amen.' Its form was Christian, but she thought about it now and its spirit seemed to her more like a true Mohawk prayer. It was like the six annual festivals held at the other longhouses on the reserve. (The Mohawks were supposed to be Christians so their own longhouse had been destroyed.) The festivals were held according to the moon and their purpose was to thank the Creator for the seasons and for the ripening of each crop as it came on. This was her